STUDENT

The Author

James Thornhill has 20 years experience in the youth media market, as founder and Editor-in-Chief of *The National Student,* the UK's first national publication for higher education students and Head of Communications at a youth marketing agency. Going freelance in 2017, James now works as a media and marketing consultant and culture journalist for many publications.

© James Thornhill 2012, 2020

Previously published in a larger format as
Student Manual in 2021.
This updated edition printed in 2020
James Thornhill has asserted his right to be
identified as the author of this work.

British Library Cataloguing in Publication Data
A catalogue record for this book is available
from the British Library.

ISBN 978 1 78521 695 4

Library of Congress catalog card no.
2019949677

Published by Haynes Publishing,
Sparkford, Yeovil, Somerset BA22 7JJ, UK
Tel: 01963 440635
Int. tel: +44 1963 440635
Website: www.haynes.com

Haynes North America Inc.
859 Lawrence Drive, Newbury Park,
California 91320, USA

Printed and bound in Malaysia

While every effort is taken to ensure the
accuracy of the information given in this book,
no liability can be accepted by the author or
publishers for any loss, damage or injury
caused by errors in, or omissions from the
information given.

ACKNOWLEDGEMENTS

Thanks to everyone who made the 17-year
history of *The National Student* such an
amazing journey, you all know who you
are. I would like to thank my parents for
their constant encouragement and
support, and Julie Yates for her motivation
while writing this book.

Special thanks must go to everyone who
helped with the completion of this book.

STUDENT

ALL YOU NEED TO KNOW IN ONE CONCISE MANUAL

James Thornhill

Contents

Introduction

To use the age-old cliché, university really is the 'time of your life'. The independence and freedom from routine, the new friends, discounts and partying, focusing on the subject you love – it's a sweet existence.

That's not to say, however, that students don't have their problems. With all the new-found freedom and independence comes a new set of responsibilities, things you may never have had to think about before. How do you turn that pile of smelly clothes in the corner into clean, crisp garments ready to wear? How do you feed yourself? How do you make your money last the whole semester? These things all seem really easy, once you have the answer. Before that it can feel like the most complicated thing in the world.

On top of all this there's the little matter of studying and using your degree to get a job. Where to start can seem like a huge mountain to climb.

The fact is that many students are just too embarrassed or proud to ask these simple questions (people like to appear as if they know it all, especially when trying to impress new-found uni friends), which is where this manual comes in. Ideally start reading it before you set off to uni, but take it with you too, as it will give you plenty of info to help you survive and thrive on campus, throughout your course, and beyond.

Chapter 1
Living

Arriving at university is daunting. Remember what your first day at school was like – the new people, the new buildings, the new teachers and the new way of doing things? It's nerve-wracking. Your parents aren't coming back for you at the end of the day, you're not going home, there's no escape – you're stuck there! Welcome to your new home ...

← The Hawthorns
← Arts
← Social Sciences
← The Refectory
← Chaplaincy Centre

Queen's Building →
Biomedical Sciences →
Mathematics →
Chemistry →

University of
BRISTOL

UNIVERSITY WALK

www.bristol.ac.uk

Freshers' Week: dos and don'ts

While Freshers' Week (the first week on campus) can be quite scary, it's also completely brilliant and exciting. The first day: room unpacked, knowing no one – for the first time ever completely unsure what's going to happen next, with no safety net to fall back on. What I did was run around the halls of residence knocking on doors to see who was behind them. Within 15 minutes I was drinking vodka with the guys upstairs – this, for me, is what Freshers' Week is all about.

It's important that you make the most of your Freshers' Week. You'll never get that time back, and done right it can be 100% the most thrilling week of your life. Here are a few tips on how to make the most of, and stay safe during, that first week:

■ DO MEET PEOPLE

You're all in the same boat. Talk to new people you'd never usually chat to. Sure, some of them won't be your friends at the end of uni, but others will become great, lasting friends. The guy across the hall turned out to be a 'dancing monster' in the band Misty's Big Adventure (I did some memorable radio shows with him); another guy who jumped on me on my first trip to the local cinema would leave weird mix tapes of strange music at my door. It's these people that make uni what it is. So it's simple – just meet people! They are what make uni amazing.

■ DO STEP OUTSIDE YOUR COMFORT ZONE

There's no better time in your life to reinvent yourself and try new things. Try stuff that you hadn't considered trying before – you might find something you're really into. You never know, you might be a secret medieval role-play fanatic, or have been simply waiting for an opportunity to unleash your inner Goth. Give things a go!

■ DON'T BE SHY

Trust me, everyone is feeling as nervous as you are. Be the one to break through the awkward silence and introduce yourself – it will make your life, and the lives of everyone around you, much easier. Don't be afraid to ask people questions to help you navigate your way around the campus and the town.

■ DO SEE WHAT YOUR UNIVERSITY HAS TO OFFER

It can be really easy to find a few places you like and stick to them, but make sure you check out everything that your university has to offer, both for socialising and to help you with your course and life. Enquire about what services are available to you, and make sure you're clued up enough to get the most out of university life.

■ DON'T BE PRESSURED INTO THINGS

While you definitely should try new things, don't allow yourself to be pressured into things you don't want to do – the satanic ritual going on in your kitchen might not be for you, so don't get involved. On a more serious note this advice applies massively to drink and drugs. Don't be coerced into taking anything you're not happy putting in your body. Your friends might suggest it's 'awesome' to neck that pint of vodka before snorting a line of coke, but if you don't want to get involved *don't*! Likewise with sports club initiation ceremonies, which are talked about later in the book. Don't do anything you don't want to do to gain acceptance. It's not worth it.

■ DO GET CLUED UP ON YOUR COURSE

During this first week your course is likely to be bottom of your agenda, but do make sure you have the basics down. Find out where and when you need to turn up, what stuff you need for the course, get an idea of the workload and hand-in dates for work. This takes no time at all and is really quite essential to setting you on the right path. There's nothing worse than failing later on because you had no idea what you were supposed to do.

■ DON'T SPLASH ALL YOUR CASH AT ONCE

That first loan payment will seem like a lot of cash – probably more than you'll have ever been given in one go. A spending spree will be really, and I mean really, tempting. A few big nights out, some new clothes and a few other treats aren't going to hurt – or so you might think! That's until you realise you haven't paid your rent, or considered other little things like eating. It's not uncommon for students to blow their loan in the first week and then struggle to pay for the important stuff.

This is particularly a problem for freshers during Freshers' Week – make sure you have all your payments considered and covered. Once this is done the rest of the cash is yours to play with.

■ DO PLAY IT SAFE

You'll get caught up in the excitement of it all, but remember that you're in a new place and consider your safety. It's best to walk round at night in groups, and to get into pre-booked or clearly registered taxis after a night out. In halls, lock your doors and windows when you go out, and don't let anyone you don't know through the door to your halls – there have been plenty of thefts in university halls. There's no need to be paranoid, but it's worth making things as safe as they can be.

REGISTER WITH A GP

When you get to uni you will need to sign up with a GP – they are kinda useful when you are feeling a bit ill! In most cases, as a student you will have access to your campus medical centre who will have a team of doctors and nurses to help you with your ailments.

If you can't get access to an on-campus medical centre you will need to sign up with a local GP. Your university should have a list of these and be able to point you in the right direction.

To register with a GP you will need to fill out a GMS1 form giving your name and address, date of birth, NHS number (if you know it) and the address of your previous GP (so they can get your medical history). Some surgeries will also ask for some sort of proof of identity. Once you are registered you will be contacted to go in for a health check within six months – to make sure you are in good working order. After this you are all good to go, and can make an appointment when you need one.

Don't be coerced into taking anything you're not happy putting in your body. Your friends might suggest it's 'awesome' to neck that pint of vodka before snorting a line of coke, but if you don't want to get involved don't!

Safety on campus

The uni bubble is a relatively safe space – most campuses have really low crime rates compared to the 'outside world'. However, accidents, assaults and thefts do occasionally happen on campus, and certainly out in town, so it pays to be aware of your surroundings and to follow these tips to help you avoid bad situations.

■ KNOW YOUR WAY AROUND

This might sound patronising but hear me out. Get the lie of the land, so you know where you are and where you are going. Otherwise, once you're drunk and in the dark you could inadvertently find yourself somewhere you don't want to be. Get to know the local area both on campus and around town while you're sober and it's light.

■ PRE-BOOK YOUR TAXI

If you can book a taxi from a reputable firm to pick you up at certain place at a certain time then do it! These days, many companies, not just Uber, have apps through which you can book and track your cab. These usually tell you the vehicle's registration and the name of the driver. Whatever you do, never get in any unmarked vehicle that offers you a lift – no matter how easy and cheap it might seem.

■ TRAVEL IN GROUPS

People are much less likely to bother big groups of people, or even just two people, so there's safety in numbers. What's more, travelling with other people will possibly help you avoid the sort of trouble you may cause yourself if you're really drunk, and hopefully they'll ensure you get home safe, if not altogether sound!

■ CARRY FEWER VALUABLES

If you've got fewer valuables on you, you'll be less of a target for thieves. Simple.

■ LOCK YOUR DOORS AND WINDOWS

Thefts do occur on campus, especially in flats located on the ground floor. It sounds obvious, but don't leave your windows open and unlocked when you go out, and also lock your doors. If no one can get in, nothing will happen. And, although you might trust your flat mates, it's likely that you won't know them properly at first, so don't take chances – lock your bedroom door.

■ DON'T LET PEOPLE IN

An old con trick is to ring all the intercoms on a block of flats and see if anyone will just open the door. Once the person has gained access they can then steal or damage property or attack someone. So, don't let anyone you don't recognise into the block and certainly not into your flat, and demand to see paperwork if they say they are from, e.g. a utilities company.

Most of the above is common sense and isn't meant to make you feel paranoid about leaving the house. However, simply thinking about what you're doing and taking precautions as a natural part of your day will help ensure nothing bad ever does happen.

Living in the uni bubble

Living on campus isn't like living in the real world. Sure, it's a step closer to being 100% responsible for yourself, but when you're living on campus everything is geared towards making your life as comfortable and easy as possible. Many of the perils of living in the real world are deflected by a shield of services and structures – like a force-field or protective bubble. As a student you're living inside the 'university bubble'.

More than any other time in your life you'll be surrounded by like-minded people, most of them the same age as you. This coupled with more freedom and free time will enable you to develop more friendships and interests than you'll ever have again.

Also, university life is geared to nurture these friendships by providing many things to do, from club nights to societies for just about anything you can think of. University is the best time to embrace your interests and make friends with people similar to yourself.

Campus life

You might be under the impression that your timetable is ridiculously hectic and jam-packed, but in all honesty you'll never again have the same kind of freedom and flexibility to work at your own pace and fit your work obligations around what you want to do with your life. In some cases you might get as little as six hours' scheduled teaching time spread over an entire week (that's less than one full working day). So while at university you should savour the freedom and the late starts (in the real world you'll be starting at 9:00am, or earlier, every day, and the place you need to be won't be on your doorstep).

Plus on bigger campuses you could probably get away with living your life almost entirely in the safe confines of the uni bubble. You have your own shops, restaurants, bars and clubs all aimed at giving you what you want in a safe environment.

On top of this everything else is positioned to make your life easier – at no other point in life will you have such easy access to support when you need it, whether it's for your health (most universities have their own medical centre),

Basically, if you're having trouble there's someone on campus whose job it is to help you. This is something that's not always readily available once you graduate.

academic worries, housing woes or other legal issues. Even if you have money worries there are people to help you out of the hole. Basically, if you're having trouble there's someone on campus whose job it is to help you. This is something that's not always readily available once you graduate.

Inside the university bubble finding somewhere to live couldn't be easier. In your first year you'll more than likely be with all the other freshers in the university halls of residence, a self-contained student estate. After that, if you're forced to venture out into the real-world housing wilderness your university will have a list of recommended landlords and agents and may even help you and your mates secure a place. If none of this works there are loads of private companies that offer private halls of residence close to campus at reasonable prices.

The campus is also generally a much safer place than the outside world. It will have its own security and CCTV network, and most fire alarms are linked to the local fire station for a quick response if anything catches fire. The powers that be want to keep you as safe as possible.

While you may have a small budget to work with and be amassing some serious debt, your actual living costs while you're studying are generally much more reasonable than for everyone else. Your students' union card will grab you some nice discounts on everything from food and clothes to Netflix and other things you don't really need. Also, as a student your rent, bills and the like will be cheaper than after you graduate. As a student you're also exempt from Council Tax (another nice saving). Your cash goes much further, so be careful with it and you should survive nicely – it just won't be a luxurious existence.

So, in short, as a student you're lucky enough to live in a bubble that's aimed at protecting you and making your life as easy as possible. You should definitely enjoy this amazing time as best you can. The rest of this book is aimed at providing tips on how to make the most of living in the university bubble.

Students' union

If there's one organisation that's central to your life as a student it's your students' union (SU). In most cases the minute you start university you become a member of your union. Essentially, they're the people who are there to make your student life better, providing the services and support you require on campus.

The students' union offers so much more than cheap drinks in their bar, although let's not knock the cheap drinks (who doesn't like cheap drinks?). It's your campaigning, political organisation which in most cases is the regional, grass-roots wing of the NUS, who they join to fight for student rights nationally.

As democratic organisations the people in charge are chosen by you, through elections. Unfortunately, turnouts for SU elections have been tradionally tragically low at most universities, with some campuses showing a low percentage of

students having their say. In some cases the elections have become a bit of a joke, with most people believing they're little more than popularity contests, with the winner getting the position due to the number of friends they have, and not how good they are for the job.

Your SU will be made up of the following people:

■ FULL-TIME ELECTED SABBATICAL OFFICERS

These are usually recent graduates from the university who take on these full-time, paid positions for one year (sometimes more if they're re-elected). The number of paid sabbaticals and the positions they hold vary from one uni to the next, but the president (the SU top dog) is usually one of them.

■ PART-TIME ELECTED OFFICERS

Students fill a variety of positions working for you on a part-time basis. These officers work for the SU on top of their studies and are often the people who go on to the full-time sabbatical positions.

■ NON-STUDENT FULL-TIME STAFF

Let's face it, students and recent graduates probably don't have all the skills and experience necessary to run an organisation with a fully functional office and a budget of millions! Because of this most SUs have non-student, full-time staff such as office managers, secretaries, accountants and marketing managers to keep the whole shebang running smoothly.

So, what do all these staff do for you?

■ REPRESENT YOU

Your SU is your voice. They're there to speak on your behalf and represent you to the university, the local community and on a national level. They're the official body that exists to make sure you and other students are heard – even if it's to criticise the work they're doing, they're there to listen and represent your grievances.

Remember that they work for you, and represent you – so if you're unhappy with them they're obliged to listen and do better!

More than 95% of students' unions affliate to the NUS, both because of the support and financial benefits they gain from being part of such a large, national organisation, and because they feel that it's important to have a national voice arguing the case of students.

■ SUPPORT YOU

Having a problem with your course, student house or something else? Students' unions provide an array of support services covering academic, housing, health and also legal issues, so if you have a problem they'll probably have a service that can help. It's their job to be on your side.

■ GIVE YOU STUFF TO SPEND YOUR CASH ON

The shop you buy your milk, sweets and magazines in on campus is usually run by the students' union. Everything in it should be at a much better price than other shops. Also, the SU will have their own cafes and bars, which should also be the most wallet-friendly places to eat and drink.

■ HELP YOUR SOCIAL LIFE

Whether it's providing cheap booze in the bars, or giving you the club nights and live music you want on your doorstep, the SU are in charge of arranging it. If you want to promote your own night on campus you'll also have to go through them. The SU are also in charge of all the sports clubs and other societies on campus. In short, anything that's official and fun on campus is down to your students' union.

■ PROVIDE YOUR OWN MEDIA

In most cases the student media on campus (radio, print, online and video) is controlled by the SU. They're in charge of providing the facilities, legal support and funding for keeping you informed about what's going on in studentland.

What does the NUS actually do?

So, you've got that lovely little discount card in your pocket – and you know your SU is part of it – but what does the National Union of Students (NUS) actually do? It's a question I get asked a lot by students. With that in mind I got the people over at NUS to give me the low-down on who they are and the work that they do. It turns out that some big changes are happening at the moment, as the NUS explain:

'Created in 1922, NUS is a confederation of students' unions giving national voice to students. It has the aim of "making education and our world better through the collective power of students", with the body growing over the years to represent

around 7 million students in higher and further education, with 95 per cent of students' unions affiliated to it.

As NUS approaches its 100th birthday it is reforming to better reflect the society it supports now, becoming two organisations with the same shared heart, but two separate, distinct and different purposes.

NUS UK will continue as a national campaigning organisation, continuing to deliver change, not just for students, but for everyone. It will, however, shift from being a policy-lobbying led organisation to being content-campaign led, involving as many students, supporters, partners and the public as possible.

Policy and lobbying will still be very much part of what it does, but its ambition is to reflect the society we live in, building a movement, engaging thousands, if not millions, of students and their supporters in its campaigns.

Building on previous achievements in higher education funding, student finance, standards and affordability in student accommodation, and transport costs, NUS UK will continue to seek solutions to the mental health crisis in further and higher education, champion the rights of apprentices and those in FE colleges, reduce the attainment gaps for students of colour, and much else besides, as it campaigns to win change across England, Scotland, Northern Ireland and Wales.

A recent example of its new approach is the general election campaign delivered in November and December 2019, working with the Electoral Commission and Hey Savvy to get as many students as possible registered to vote, informed on their voting options and voting. Over 2.6 million young people registered for this

election compared to 1.4 million in 2017, with nearly half a million taking advantage of NUS' VoteSavvy app. The digital tool provided an assessment of party manifestos against students' concerns enabling each user to see which party best aligned to their values.

Although this increase wasn't all down to NUS, by building channels that connect to its campaigners, the people it's trying to influence, and the public, it believes it can win the change it wants to see.

Student leadership is the primary strength and the NUS continue to build connections between its student leaders and the students they represent. NUS UK's seven full-time officer executive team is elected by five conferences – one for each nation plus Liberation, encompassing minority group campaigns (black students, woman students, LGBT+ students, trans students and disabled students). Taking up office for a two-year period, beginning on 1 July 2020, the officer executive team will translate the policy discussed, debated and agreed at

NUS National Conference, involving nearly 1,000 students, into an annual campaign Plan for Action.

Any student or student officer can run to stand for any of NUS UK's elected positions or get involved in its campaigns, but the easiest way to do this is through the students' union at their university or college. NUS UK's sister organisation, NUS Charitable Services, will therefore aim to support students through the provision of a strong students' union for every student, making the case for students' unions and championing their stand-alone value.

Strong students' unions are integral to delivering a powerful student voice, locally and nationally, so NUS Charitable Services will be the leading voice for the students' union sector in relation to government policies, charity governance and legislation. It will work to be the leading membership support organisation for students' unions, and their appointed and elected leaders, and will provide up-to-date and relevant information, advice and guidance on matters of major importance to students' unions.

NUS Charitable Services will continue to provide services and partnerships to benefit students and attract talent from outside the student movement. It will celebrate diversity in employment and enable students' unions to evolve as social enterprises providing social value and better outcomes for students.

It will champion the students' union brand, positioning the sector as an employer of choice for diverse talent and cultivate income generation potential, enabling students' unions to evolve as social enterprises providing social value and better outcomes for students.'

In short, the NUS are YOUR voice on the issues that matter to you and so much more than just the people who give you a discount card!

Student committees

Maybe you don't want to get involved in the students' union but still want to be involved in helping students have a voice within the union and the university. If so, you need to get involved in student committees.

The various types of student committee tend to represent specific student groups, such as course subjects, or things like certain disabilities.

These can be organised on a course, college or halls basis depending on the structure of the university you attend.

Most universities have a Students' Union Council that gives student representatives an all-important platform to oversee and question (if necessary) the work of the students' union officers and sabbaticals. Members get the chance to grill officers at organised meetings and also mandate them to take action on the issues that matter (basically force them to act). Union councils have a range of responsibilities such as planning union budgets, setting up select

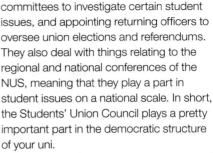

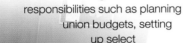

committees to investigate certain student issues, and appointing returning officers to oversee union elections and referendums. They also deal with things relating to the regional and national conferences of the NUS, meaning that they play a part in student issues on a national scale. In short, the Students' Union Council plays a pretty important part in the democratic structure of your uni.

Some of the different groups represented in student committees are BAME Students, International Students, LGBT Students (Lesbian, Gay, Bisexual and Trans Students), Mature Students, Postgraduate Taught, Postgraduate Research Students, Students with Disabilities, and Women. Most of student life is represented in some way, meaning that if you have an issue you can normally get yourself heard.

The committees are usually made up of the most dedicated students, and if you want to be a committee member dedication is what you need! Once you hold a committee position you might be approached by any number of students with any number of different problems and issues, so make sure you're willing to commit before taking the decision to join one.

There tend to be elections for presidents of committees, but for general positions you can usually get involved at any point during the year. You can also leave if you feel that you're not able to devote the necessary amount of time to the committee.

You should enquire with your students' union about what committees operate within your campus. Most committees will also have web pages where you'll be able to find contact details of those already involved.

Chapter 2
Not going broke

Going to university is likely to be the first time you need to learn the true value of money, the first time you'll need to manage paying for everything – rent, food, going out ... everything! And it's all coming out of your pocket.

What does going to uni cost?

There's no doubt that university costs a lot more now than it used to. Those Baby Boomers heading up the company you want to work for likely got their further education for free – before 1998 it cost nothing and you also received a grant to live off. Since then, if you happen to study in England, the fees have risen greatly, and grants have all but disappeared. The fact remains, though, that in order to embark on many careers you still need to get a degree. So, how do you pay for it?

To make matters worse for potential students, there's a lot of misinformation, myth and misunderstanding about the finance system floating around, and this can be both off-putting and confusing. Let's clarify the situation. Not everywhere in the UK has the same rules, and some regions certainly have a better deal than others. Here are the differences between the four home nations.

- **England** – People studying in England really do get the short end of the tuition fee stick. Universities can charge up to £9,250 per year for all UK and EU students. For accelerated degrees – those that are condensed into a shorter time – they can charge a massive £11,100 per year. Around 76 per cent of universities charge the full amount.

- **Wales** – Undergraduates in Wales get a slightly better deal than those in England, with fees of up to £9,000 a year. You won't have to pay the fees upfront.

- **Northern Ireland** – You'll get charged anything up to £4,275 per year to study in Northern Ireland. This is not paid upfront.

- **Scotland** – The fee system in Scotland has been causing quite a bit of controversy, with English students shouting about how unfair the system is. If you are a Scottish student you can still get your university education for free in Scotland. However, all non-Scottish UK students have to pay the full amount if they opt to study there.

A SLIDING SCALE

It was in September 2012 that universities got the right to charge up to £9,250 per year in tuition fees for full-time undergraduate study, rising from £3,375 per year. That said, many colleges and smaller universities charge considerably less in order to attract more students, so it's definitely worth considering them if they offer a course you may want to do.

Student loans

Wherever you choose to go to uni, compared to the Boomers who got it all for free, your studies are going to cost you a fortune. It's enough to put anyone off.

But don't despair: help is at hand in the form of a student loan. Yes, you'll have to pay it back, but taking a loan will mean you can afford university and hopefully progress to the career of your dreams.

If you are about to start university you will have, more than likely, already sorted out your loan with the Student Loans Company (the government-run body responsible for lending you the money, and getting it back). However, if you are starting in a year or so then you will still need to apply. There are two types of loan you can get your mitts on:

1 A tuition fee loan

This type of loan covers the fees you are charged to attend university. This loan is paid directly to your university or college.

MAXIMUM TUITION FEE LOANS (2019/20)

Student type	Tuition Fee Loan
New full-time students	£9,250
New full-time students on accelerated degrees	£11,100
New full-time students at private university or college	£6,165
New part-time students	£6,935
New part-time students at private university or college	£4,625

2 A maintenance loan

This loan is the one most people are talking about when they talk about your 'student loan'. It helps you with your living costs, or, if you are less than sensible, the acquisition of a massive pile of new shoes. The amount you can borrow depends on a number of

things, such as where you live, how much your folks earn and what year of uni you are in. You will get this at the start of each term, in one go. So don't spend it all at once because once it is gone, it is really gone!

MAXIMUM MAINTENANCE LOAN RATES FOR FULL-TIME STUDENTS 2019/20

Where you live and study	Maintenance Loan
You live at home	£7,529
You live away from home and study outside London	£8,944
You live away from home and study in London	£11,672
You spend a year of a UK course studying overseas	£10,242

Before you can get any of this financial help you'll have to prove that you are eligible for a loan based on all the factors mentioned above. You can get the full low-down on what you will need to prove and provide by contacting your regional student finance office. It might all sound quite complicated but staff at these offices should be able to help you with the application process. You can contact the following offices for more information:

- **England –** www.direct.gov.uk/StudentFinance
- **Scotland –** www.saas.gov.uk
- **Wales –** www.studentfinancewales.co.uk or www.cyllidmyfyrwyrcymru.co.uk
- **Northern Ireland –** www.studentfinanceni.co.uk

You can also visit the Student Loans Company website: www.slc.co.uk

Payback time

The downside to all this borrowing is that you will eventually probably have to pay it back. Full-time students will need to start making repayments the April after the course finishes, while part-time students start repayment the April four years after the course start date. However, this timeframe is dependent on income: you won't need to pay a penny back until you're earning £25,725 in England and Wales, and £18,935 in Scotland and Northern Ireland. What's more, if you haven't managed to pay back the loan in full after 30 years it will be wiped out. This sounds like a great thing, but in reality if you have not earned enough to pay back the loan in that time then chances are your income will be very low. Not such a win after all!

The amount you pay back once your income exceeds these thresholds is a proportion of your salary, so to start with the payments will be fairly small and affordable, increasing as your salary (hopefully) goes up. At present, you will pay back 9 per cent of what you earn over £25,725, and this rate remains the same no matter what you earn or how much you borrowed. You can always choose to pay more at any time to help clear your debts quicker, but this is the basic deal. And, although the government can change these details at any time they like, they usually make an announcement in plenty of time.

TYPICAL STUDENT LOAN REPAYMENTS FOR VARIOUS SALARIES

Yearly income before tax	Monthly income before tax	Monthly repayment
£25,725	£2,143	£0
£27,000	£2,250	£9
£29,500	£2,458	£28
£31,000	£2,583	£39
£33,000	£2,750	£55

Source: UCAS

Getting a student bank account

You'll be needing somewhere to stash that loan (and other) cash, and in the lead-up to starting university a load of banks will no doubt have been doing their best to entice you to store it with them. Yes, sorry, you do need to have a bank account.

Banks will have offered you all sorts of treats to get your business, but forget about that free pen and think about what's going to be best for you to get the most out of your cash.

Here are a few things to think about when you're choosing your account:

What's the limit?

Hello, student, meet Overdraft. Overdraft is your new best friend!

Seriously, as a student you'll live off your overdraft, and it's literally a lifesaver. When all those nights out have added up, and you're dangerously close to having spent every penny you have, your overdraft will allow you to keep drawing out money (and spending).

Your overdraft is the facility that allows you to keep spending even after your account has reached £0. Most student bank accounts offer an overdraft of between £1,000 and £3,000. Even better, unlike normal accounts the bank won't even charge you interest on what you take out.

But don't see this as free money. Drawing out £1,000 from your overdraft will mean sticking that amount back in just to get back to nought. And you do have to pay this money back eventually. When you graduate your bank will phase out the overdraft being interest free, so the longer you're using your overdraft the

more money you'll end up paying to the bank for the privilege. Only use your overdraft when you have to. If you don't have any money to go out or buy a new pair of jeans, stay in and wear your old ones. If you don't have enough money for food, however, by all means use your overdraft. Keep expenditure down to a minimum, however.

When comparing bank accounts you should check out which have the best overdraft limits, and read the terms carefully to find out what the interest level is if you go past your overdraft limit (that's

the point at which you exceed your agreed limit). Some banks charge close to 20%, or expect a fee of a few pounds to be paid every so often until you go back up into the 0% interest zone. Everyone makes mistakes, and you don't want to spiral further into debt because of harsh overdraft charges.

Check the perks

So, in reality the perks offered by banks are a little more enticing than a free pen. In fact some of them are pretty sweet. See what each bank is willing to give you for signing with them. Each year there's a nice array of little bribes on offer – a free Young Person's Railcard, contents insurance, cash and even Netflix subscriptions have all been put on offer. While this shouldn't be the only thing you base your decision on, it can certainly make the decision easier.

Read the contract

You've decided on an account with a good deal on an overdraft and a perk, but don't rush to stick your signature on the dotted line just yet. Check over the contract first and ask the following questions:

- Is there a minimum amount I need to open the account (and do I have it)?
- Is there a monthly or annual charge for keeping the account?
- Do any charges come into effect if I go into my overdraft, or if my account goes lower than a certain amount?
- Can the 0% interest overdraft limit be increased? If so, what's the maximum?
- Will I get a credit card when signing up for the account?
- Are there any rules about how much I need to use the account – are there a certain number of deposits and withdrawals I need to make each month?

What the banks offer

Your bank, too, can probably help you out financially. This is what the biggest banks were offering to students at the time of writing this book:

Lloyds TSB

- **Overdraft** – £1,500 interest-free during years one to three. If you study for longer the overdraft is increased to £2,000 for years four to six.
- **Contactless debit card**
- **Internet banking**
- **Mobile app and payments** – Banking app available on iOS and Android, simple mobile payments via Apple Pay and Google Pay.
- **Perks** – Lloyds offer 15 per cent cashback on purchases from selected retailers, such as Hilton, the Co-op, Costa and Sky.

Barclays

- **Overdraft** – £500 on opening an account, going up to £3,000 while you are studying. This is all fee-free.
- **Personalised debit card** – You can stick your own face on it, or that of a pet, or anything really.
- **Barclays banking app** – Control your account from your device and send money quickly and safely with Pingit.
- **Perks** – Cashback on purchases from selected retailers online and on the high street.
  – Three free textbooks for first year students when you sign up with the Campus Society and take a Barclays Student Additions Account.

HSBC

- **Overdraft** – £1,000 in year one, with an increase up to £3,000 by year three.
- **Banking app and online banking**
- **Bill splitting through Paym as part of the app**
- **Options to open Regular Saver or Loyalty ISAs**
- **Perks** – Student-exclusive discounts with places such as Boohoo, Apple and Revolution Bars – £100 for first year students signing up before 31 December (they run offers like this regularly).

Santander

- **Overdraft** – Fee-arranged overdraft in the first three years of £1,500–£1,800 in year 4 and £2,000 if you study for a fifth year (or more).
- **Online and mobile banking**
- **Monthly interest of 3 per cent AER/2.96 per cent gross (variable) on balances from £300 up to a maximum of £2,000.**
- **Perks** – a free four-year 16–25 Railcard to save one-third on rail travel in Great Britain.
  - 15 per cent cashback at a range of major retailers.
  - Offers on their 1|2|3 World financial services, such as travel insurance and ISAs.

Halifax

- **Overdraft** – Fee-arranged overdraft of up to £1,500 for the duration of your course and for the first year after you graduate (up to a maximum of six years).
- **Contactless Visa debit card**
- **Online and mobile banking**
- **Eligible for Save The Change** – With this, Halifax will round up any debit card payment and pay the difference into a savings account. For example, if a coffee costs £2.20, 80p will be paid into your savings account.
- **Perks** – Cashback on big brands with their Cashback Extras when you register for online banking.

NatWest

- **Overdraft** – An interest-free overdraft of up to £2,000, with £500 in the first term. You can get an instant online decision for this.
- **Mobile banking app**
- **Perks** – Choose between either an Amazon Prime Student membership, a National Express Coachcard or a tastecard.

This is what is on offer from the big traditional banks right now, but be aware that app-based banks such as Starling and Monzo are shaking up the industry, offering products with stronger budgeting built in. It is therefore worth looking into what these new banks can offer in this ever-changing industry.

The art of budgeting

You've got your cash safely stored in a bank, now you need to make it pay for everything you need. Ensuring that you have enough to not fall short on important payments, while still having fun, is the goal.

Even if you try to get by on just instant noodles and only wash your clothes once a month, things still cost money, so you need to know exactly what you need to spend each month. This is where budgeting comes in.

Fortunately for you, it's never been easier to do. Many banking apps have an in-built budgeting functions these days, and there is a long list of other apps that make is simple to see what you are spending and how much you have left. These are some of the apps available:

■ Money Dashboard
■ Bean
■ Emma
■ Mint
■ Pocket Guard

How to write a budget

If you prefer not to use technology you can simply write down a list of outgoings (money going out), detailing dates and amounts. Known costs can include:

■ **Rent and other accommodation costs**
■ **Utility bills** – Stuff like water, electricity and gas. These may be included in your rent and accommodation costs. If they're not, don't forget to factor them in, allowing a little extra for contingency.

- **Phone bills**
- **Internet costs**
- **Laundry** – Whether you use coin machines in uni (or off campus) or your own washing machine at home, there are costs to consider, such as washing powder etc.
- **Insurance** – Both for your possessions and, if you have one, your car.
- **Travel** – Stuff like bus passes, train tickets and petrol.
- **Food** – You need to make sure you can afford to eat. Meals will be covered if you are living in catered halls of residence – and included in the bill – but if not then you really need to get your head around how much a weekly shop costs.

After you have listed your outgoings, add up how much money you will have coming in for the same period, including your student loan, bank overdraft, any income from a job and any help from your parents. Then subtract the cost of what you need to spend from the amount you have in your account to see how much money you have left to play with. Yes, doing this is a bit scary but it is much better than burying your head in the sand and running out of cash.

With the amount you have left over you can work out what you can spend on other things, such as:

- **Toiletries and cleaning products** – All the stuff you need to keep both you and your digs clean and looking pretty.
- **Clothes** – You might like to buy yourself something fashionable, every once in a while.
- **Going out** – Socialising is an

important part of being at uni but it can easily be the thing that makes you run out of cash.

- **Holidays** – All that studying can be stressful and you might like a nice holiday in the sun to unwind. These are not cheap, though, so you will need to really be on top of your finances to afford a trip to sunny climes rather than Skegness! You may also realise that you in fact need to spend the holidays working in order to fund the extras during term time.

You can go back and amend your budget if you find that stuff costs more (or less) than you thought. If, at the end of the process you discover that you'll only have £5 to live on each week, try to find ways to slim down your costs, such as changing your phone contract or buying second-hand books rather than new ones. You may also need to think about getting a part-time job during term time. Going past your bank overdraft limit can only add to your expenses, so try your best to live off what you've got.

Other grants and allowances

Maintenance Grant

This is like the Maintenance Loan except that you don't have to pay it back! As such, it is the holy grail of student finance. Sadly for those going to uni in England, however, you can no longer apply for it. Sorry. Elsewhere, depending on what your folks earn and where you study you can grab up to £3,475 a year in Northern Ireland, and at least £1,000 a year in Wales. In Scotland, the Young Students' Bursary gives up to £1,875 a year. NB: anything you get as a grant will reduce the loan you can receive, so you'll have the same amount of money, but won't have to pay back quite so much.

Special Support Grant

If your family gets Income Support or Housing Benefit (including the housing element of Universal Credit) then you might be able to get a Special Support Grant instead of the Maintenance Grant. It's pretty much the same as the Maintenance Grant, but it won't affect the amount you get for your Maintenance Loan, effectively meaning it's additional cash.

Disabled Students Allowances (DSAs)

There's a range of financial support available for people with physical, mental health and learning disabilities in order to help them succeed in their studies. If you are eligible, you can dip into the following as a full-time student starting in 2020:

- **Non-medical helper's allowance** – Up to £23,258 per academic year.
- **Specialist equipment allowance** – Maximum of £5,849 per academic year.

- **General allowance** – Maximum of £1,954 per academic year.
- **Travel allowance** – Amount varies depending on disability.

NHS Bursary

In the past, the NHS Bursary helped students taking healthcare degrees across the UK, but it's now a complicated patchwork of financial support (too complicated and extensive to cover here) depending on which country you are from and where you are studying. Still, these bursaries exist to help you into the medical profession, so look into what is available to you.

Scholarships and awards

Different from grants, these are given out for outstanding achievements instead of being based on income. There are numerous such schemes so it is worth doing your research if you think you stand a chance of winning one.

Student hardship fund

If you're not managing to make ends meet, you might be eligible for a hardship fund. There is a chance that this will be given to you as another loan but you could also be lucky enough to get it as a grant (i.e. something you don't have to pay back). You can usually apply for hardship funds more than once in a university year, but each university will have a different process to follow and the requirements you need to meet to get some cash differ as well. Based on income and essential expenditure, you could get anything from £100 to £3,000.

Moneymaking ideas

No matter how careful you are with your money, everyone could always do with a little more to spend (unless you're Jeff Bezos). Other than doing the obvious thing and getting a part-time job, here are a few other ideas to help you make a few extra quid.

Work at open days

Most universities have open days at which they sell the uni and campus to new students. Who better to show them round than current students? If you can talk to strangers for a few hours then you can make some fairly decent money. Keep an eye out on campus for postings about this job or visit your campus' marketing department to see if they have more details.

Sell your stuff online

It's amazing what some people want, and what they are willing to pay good money for. When you clear out all that old stuff

If you can talk to strangers for a few hours then you can make some fairy decent money.

from the back of your wardrobe or from under your bed, don't throw it out, stick in online or on one of the many selling apps. Here are just a few:

- **eBay** – The most famous online marketplace. People bid to 'win' the privilege of buying your items from you. You will be charged for listing and they take a percentage of the sale price, but it can be well worth doing.

- **Depop** – The go-to app for selling second-hand clothes. They take 10 per cent of every sale.

- **Vinted** – Another good clothes-selling app. No fees here – the buyer pays.

- **Amazon marketplace** – Got old books and DVDs? Amazon is a great place to list your stuff as it has such a vast customer base. A selling account and listing are free, but they take a percentage of the sales price.

Buy through cashback sites

You're probably buying loads of stuff online anyway, right? So why not make some money back every time you hit Pay? Basically, you earn money simply by doing your shopping. This is a great service for students (and everyone else!).

Put on a club night

Why not ramp up your drunken gatherings with your mates a notch? Hire out a venue; many will let you have it for free on quiet nights if you guarantee a certain number through the door – they keep the bar money, you take the door money and everyone is happy. At uni you will have access to loads of friends (and other bystanders) whom you can convince to come along. Get a mate to DJ for a small fee, or free, play the music people want to hear and then charge people just a little bit on the door. If it all goes well, it could be a nice, and regular, little earner.

Busk

If you are a little bit musical then you could get out and do a bit of busking. This works well for people who are pretty good, but it is not recommended if all you can do is hit a triangle out of time.

Sell your IT know-how

Do you know your way around a computer? There will be people on campus, and off, who really don't. Especially when you are living in halls of residence, you could do quite nicely by being on call to solve people's IT issues. If you get a name for yourself as the master of all things digital then there is a chance you could find yourself with a lot of work.

Chapter 3
Finding shelter

Having somewhere to sleep and keep your stuff is pretty important! It's safe to assume that until now your parents (or some other family member) will have been providing the roof over your head, so finding shelter can seem a pretty mind-spinning task. There's a lot to consider and get your head around, but with a little bit of know-how it shouldn't be that difficult to find somewhere awesome to live.

Halls of residence – what you need to know

As a fresher it's likely that you'll be living in a halls of residence, which is basically a self-contained student community, like one of those gated communities you see rich people living in – not as posh or nice maybe, but with more parties.

Most halls of residence are run by universities, but over the past 20 years many private companies have also joined in to offer student accommodation blocks. As student numbers rose, there were too many people with not enough rooms available, so companies like Unite, Host and Fresh Student Living stepped in to fill this gap in the market. These can be quite expensive, but often offer luxury living compared to the basic student digs of old.

Basically, this is a nice buffer zone between living at home and stepping out into the real world of renting and living alone. It's the renting equivalent of learning to ride a bike with training wheels on.

Some modern and more expensive halls have a dishwasher, probably in an attempt to avoid the mounds of mouldy pots that student flats are famous for.

The living space

Regardless of the hall's set-up you'll essentially get a room with furniture, a phone, Internet access and a small en suite toilet/shower (and by 'small' I mean wardrobe sized), or a sink in older style halls.

Some older halls have rooms along vast corridors, while newer ones tend to be split into flats with a kitchen and living area per flat. If you find yourself with a room on a long corridor of student rooms the bathroom and kitchen facilities can often be shared by an entire floor.

STUDENT ROOM TYPES

Halls of residence rooms can be split down into three basic types. These can all vary in size and quality depending on where you're studying or which company you go with:

- **Standard room** – With this you get a basic room with bed, wardrobe, desk and drawers. The bathroom and kitchen facilities are used by everyone, so nothing is private for you! These can be in self-contained flats or in massive blocks with lots of rooms per floor.
- **Standard room with sink** – Basically the same as above but with a sink, so at least you can have a wash and clean your teeth without queuing.

■ **En-suite room** – Many newer rooms are en-suite (meaning you have your own bathroom – shower, sink and toilet). Of course, the en-suite varies in space, from the size of a wardrobe to an average family bathroom, depending on where you are and how much you're paying.

The kitchen tends to have the bare essentials you'll need – cooker, fridge, freezer, storage etc (some will have a microwave). Some might already have things like plates and cutlery, and other pots and pans. It's worth seeing what you'll be provided with and making sure you have everything you need in order to feed yourself. You really don't realise how useful plates are until you've tried eating your dinner off other things!

Some modern and more expensive halls have a dishwasher, probably in an attempt to avoid the mounds of mouldy pots that student flats are famous for.

Bills etc

These places like to make things easy for you. For most people it's their first time away from home, and in a bid not to overwhelm you everything is included in the cost – that's rent and bills (like water, electricity, gas, Internet etc) – so provided you pay your rent on time you should be good to go.

Keep it clean

Your parents aren't there any more, and unfortunately that means having to clean everything yourself. Some halls do have a cleaner, but not many. In the contract you'll sign universities expect a general level of cleanliness and maintenance in their halls. Despite you technically being adults and living alone, you can expect inspections every now and again to check you're not ruining the place and putting your health at risk (it does happen – just check some of the stories in the 'Renting nightmares' section on page 48). If you wipe things down, dust and hoover once in a while you should have no bother at all.

Hunting for a student house

Eventually (usually after the first year) you'll have to move out of the lovely safe bubble of halls of residence living and start renting out in the real world. You're now in the hands of landlords and letting agencies, and there's of a lot of things you can fall foul of. Unfortunately, not all landlords are nice people, and naive students are the perfect target to exploit and rip off.

The whole house-hunting process probably seems a little daunting, but by knowing where to look and what to look for there's no reason why you shouldn't be able to find an awesome place to live.

Where to start?
Your university accommodation office is a good place to start. Most will have a list of approved landlords and letting agents and they can give you the contact details for these. So in one move you can find out who to contact, and know that they're not dodgy (well, with the university's endorsement they shouldn't be).

Who to live with?
You'll no doubt choose the people you want to live with out of the people you like the most at university. But do think about

who you'll find it easiest to live with, not just the person you like going out with the most. Yes, Chris might be a laugh on a night out, but his penchant for setting fire to things and getting naked might not be the best qualities in a housemate! Make sure you move in with someone you think you can trust and will still get on with when you see them all the time.

Don't be too quick to say yes

There's always a little bit of a panic that if you don't say yes quickly all the places will go – landlords in particular will fuel your paranoia to try and get you to snap up their place. But don't panic! Take time to check out as many as possible. Yes, you might end up in the place you first viewed, and yes you might miss out on some, but without looking at as much of what's available as possible you can't be sure you've found the best home for you.

Size really does matter!

Your room in student halls probably wasn't what you'd call spacious, but it would have been designed to fit you and all your stuff in comfortably – giving you enough room to live, work and play in one space. Think about how you're going to store your stuff now. You might be able to get all your belongings into a room, but it's no good if you can't move around afterwards or get to your bed!

What's included?

Your halls room was probably furnished (a bed, wardrobe and desk at the very least). This might not be the case when you move into a private rented property. It can come as a big (and expensive shock) to find that beautiful room you looked at full of furniture is bare on moving in!

Furniture is expensive, so make sure you have checked what you are going to get in the deal.

Location, location, location

Work out exactly where the place is in relation to the things you need to use – uni, shops, pubs. You may find an awesome place out of the way, with really cheap rent, but will need to spend a fortune on taxis and buses to get to and from places (it all adds up). Look at how much this is going to cost, multiply it over a week or a month and see how much you'll have to spend on top of rent. Does it actually work out cheaper than a place closer to campus?

What's the rent?

Make sure you find out the rent and what it covers. This might seem a bit patronising to mention, but do make sure you can pay the rent. Landlords tend to get a bit, shall we say, annoyed if you don't have the cash to give them (generally that's all they care about). That price next to the pretty picture of the house is what you'll have to give them each week (or month) to stop them making you homeless. A 'pw' next to the price means that's what it costs to live in the house per week, and if you see 'pcm' it means the price per calendar month.

Watching TV? Get a licence!

If you have a television (or want to watch live television on the net) you'll need a TV licence – you'll only need one, and split between everyone in the house it doesn't work out too expensive, and certainly not as much as the fine you'll be hit with for not having one.

On top of the rent there'll be the little matter of bills (water, gas, electricity). Some landlords offer all-inclusive rent which covers all this – which is fantastic, as you'll only have to make one payment, leaving much less chance of forgetting to pay something.

If bills aren't included, ask the landlord to give you an idea of typical costs so that you can factor that into your decision of whether to take the place on.

Before moving in you'll also be expected to lay down a deposit, which is basically a payment to cover anything you might/will break or soil while living there (and in a student house, let's face it, there's a high chance of this happening). The amount can vary widely, from just a few hundred pounds to the value of one month's (or even two months') rent, depending on where in the country you are and the size of the house you're moving into. Of course, provided you don't wreck the place you should eventually get this money back.

You're paying – make sure the landlord has done their bit

Safety first! You really don't want to be moving into a house only for there to be unexpected explosions, building collapses or electrocutions a few months in. By law your landlord or letting agency has to provide you with two things when you move in – a Gas Safety Certificate showing when the boiler was last checked, and a receipt or a document showing where your security deposit is being held while renting the property (this is called the Tenancy Deposit Scheme). You should get these things straight away – if not, keep bothering them until you do.

You should also make sure that the electrical system and appliances in the property are safe, and have been checked by a PAT-registered electrician. Electrocution is at the very least painful and can be lethal, so it's well worth asking questions about the safety of wiring, appliances etc before you move in.

Getting your deposit back

Each and every year this is a huge bugbear for student renters. Landlords really, and I mean *really*, like to keep your deposit – it's essentially money for doing nothing! They'll use any excuse to keep some, or all, of your deposit – they have lots of little tricks of the trade to justify keeping an extra chunk of your cash. But follow these simple tips to make sure you have the upper hand and so get your money back.

KNOW WHAT'S ALREADY BROKEN

Know what's there and what's broken before you move in. Ask your landlord to give you an inventory of what's in the house and what condition it's in. You don't want to be held responsible for any broken doors or stained sofas when you move out.

Also, take pictures of everything and make your own list – even landlords find it hard to argue with photographic evidence (although some of them will try). Give all this to the landlord or letting agency right away, *and keep copies for yourself* – that way you've covered your back when they conveniently lose them.

CLEANLINESS IS NEXT TO GODLINESS

Give your place a really good clean. Yes, I know when you moved in it was filthy and the landlord claimed it had been 'professionally cleaned', but it's not unheard of for landlords to charge departing tenants with the cost of cleaning and then never actually have the cleaning done! The cleaner the place is when you leave the less opportunity you're providing to dodgy landlords to rip you off. Plus it's nice to leave the place in a state you'd want to move into yourself.

IT'S THE END – GET YOUR DEPOSIT BACK

Between all of you the sum of money you gave to your landlord as a deposit will be pretty huge – make sure you get it all back. If you don't ask, in many cases you won't get, and unless you've completely trashed the place you should be able to get a nice sum of money back.

Once your landlord has been round to check the place is still standing you should get your cash back within ten days of the end of the tenancy.

Follow all the tips and you should get your deposit back. That is, unless you really have broken everything and ruined the carpet, when it's safe to say you probably won't be getting a penny.

Insurance

There's every chance you won't have even considered getting insurance, but the minute anything breaks or is stolen (which does happen) you'll seriously regret not having signed up for some.

Getting insurance is very easy – you can get it just about anywhere, even your supermarket. There are even companies that specialise in insuring students, for example Endsleigh.

The key to getting the right deal on insurance is to do your research. This is not just about finding the cheapest option, but also reading the fine print to see what kind of cover is best for your needs.

Price comparison sites are really useful for this – you know the sort, the ones with those adverts on television that ingrain themselves in your mind. So just type the name from the most annoying jingle into Google and off you go. But remember, not all companies will be listed on price comparison sites (Direct Line aren't, for instance), so it'll be worth making some phone calls as well.

Never be afraid to ask questions before signing on the dotted line. While different kinds of insurance policies generally work in a similar way, it's best to know exactly what you're getting.

For your student home you'll need home contents insurance. This basically protects your property from damage and theft. So if some bugger nicks your laptop you can get some cash back to cover the loss. Contents insurance can also protect against damage from fire and water. It can even cover things that you take outside the house, such as bicycles, mobile phones and handbags.

To get this kind of insurance your house needs to have windows and doors

---

Price comparison sites are really useful for this – you know the sort, the ones with those adverts on television that ingrain themselves on your mind. So just type the name from the most annoying jingle into Google and off you go.

---

that lock (it's very unlikely that it doesn't). Check what your policy says about this – in some cases claims have been rejected because front windows didn't have locks on the handles.

Finally, check that you know *exactly* what you're covered for before taking the policy.

Renting nightmares

'Home is where the heart is'. 'There's no place like home'. 'Home Sweet Home'. All these classic sayings imply that 'home' is somewhere you should feel comfortable, safe and worry-free. Sadly, however, for some people, especially students, home can be a place of pure horror – from collapsing ceilings and dangerous chemicals to threatening landlords and nasty neighbours. But don't take my word for it. Here, some students past and present share some of their renting nightmares. Be afraid!!

Diane Jardine used to work for a landlord in Glasgow who had a particular skill for endangering students. She told me some of her most shocking stories about her unnamed employer – she didn't want to mention his name, and to be fair he does sound scary. Here are some of her best (worst) ones:

Probably the worst was the 'bleach incident'. The landlord used to hire cleaners and some of them were a bit dodgy, and he used to buy this cheap industrial-strength bleach that he made them use – the kind of stuff that strips paint off walls. One time a 'cleaner' put this bleach all over the bath and just left it, no rinsing – nothing! Some poor female student filled the bath and the bleach just diluted, she got in and it made a complete mess of her skin! With permanent scarring I think. She threatened legal action. The landlord refused to accept any responsibility for the disaster, saying it was her fault and stuff and that the cleaner hadn't been there that day. He eventually settled out of court with a wad of cash in a brown paper bag!

Another time it took him over a year to fix a broken window (some Glasgow tenements have these 'protected' type of old fancy windows) just because he'd have to get a particularly expensive type of frame for it. His solution was to put cardboard over it and Gaffer tape it on. When the tenant finally had had enough and threatened to report him over it, he was in turn threatened with violence! Needless to say, the tenant left and the window was left as it was and some other poor person was let the room with 'promises' it would get fixed. It was still broken when I quit.

In another incident, after a ceiling came down (luckily the tenant was out when it happened) the landlord refused to pay for the damage to their stuff (it had been a dodgy DIY fix that caused the collapse) saying they should have had insurance. As if that wasn't bad enough, it took months and months for him to fix it with this poor tenant living in dust and chaos for all that time with no rebate or anything. They got the usual response: 'if you don't like it, f**k off' that the landlord liked to give.

It would be nice to say that incidents like the ones Diane describe are few and far between but talk to any student renter and the stories just keep coming.

'Our contract started, and the washing machine was breaking. When it eventually broke a week after we moved in, we emailed the letting agents immediately. However, they did nothing except chase a lost cause for a month! One of my housemates started Febrezing her clothes so that she could wear them and still smell nice... Oh, and another one keeps rats. And brings them into the kitchen...' – *Andrew Fox, University of Nottingham*

'I was visiting a mate when his landlord came round to search for their gas leak using ... a LIGHTER!' – *Geraldine Kennedy-Brown, University of Birmingham*

'We have mould in our house's rooms, bathroom and living room. The estate agents don't care and two of our housemates moved out so we all had to leave in February with nowhere else to go.' – *Ella Howell, Buckinghamshire New University*

'I was in a house for two weeks and the bailiffs turned up to evict us because the landlord wasn't paying his mortgage.' – *Richard Brown, University of Birmingham*

'We had an ant infestation in the walls of our (spotless) halls kitchen. We were told to buy some ant powder on two occasions, which we did, but by the time we left they were crawling all over the walls out of holes in the ceiling.' – *Louise Oakley, De Montfort University*

And then there's poor Luke Mitchell, who suffered from a multitude of horrors in his student abode:

One place I lived was a bit of a student nightmare, on the Beavers Farm Estate in Hounslow. It was cheap. After viewing they made me leave my bag there as deposit, to prove I would come back. The front door had a head-sized hole in where the

I was visiting a mate when his landlord came round to search for their gas leak using ... a lighter!

dog – called Spliff – could pop his head out to guard for intruders. On my first day one of my fellow housemates went to prison for knocking someone down in his courier van while jumping a red under the influence. My room was full of stolen hairdressing equipment. One day I was making breakfast and was disturbed when some Aussie bloke walked in, in his pants. I'd never seen him before but, apparently, he'd lived there six months – the couple I rented with hadn't bothered to mention him. It was so close to the Heathrow runway, every three minutes my radio was interrupted by pilots.

And finally some of my own personal nightmares! I once walked downstairs one morning in just my boxer shorts, thinking the house was empty, only to find my landlord not only going through the fridge but actually making a sandwich. He was also helping himself to a cup of tea! His only explanation was that he 'owned the place' and 'had every right to be in the house'. Whatever you are told, this is not true: you are entitled to privacy – what you want to do in your own home is up to you, without the worry of having your landlord walk in unannounced.

The stories are endless, and not just about landlords. A friend from university once told me of the time he came home to find his flatmate drying metal cutlery in the microwave!!! The orange sparks coming from the microwave weren't enough for him to realise this was a bad idea...

Basic maintenance and DIY tips

Living in a house, things go wrong all the time – the heating won't come on, the lights have gone out, the toilet won't flush, and so on. You can ask your landlord to fix it, but it probably won't get done very quickly. Landlords are always slow to do everything except ask for your rent.

But don't worry, there's really no need for you to have to sit in the cold and dark, with no working toilet. In this section we'll look at some basic things you can do to keep your house working.

Water

Water's pretty essential to your house. You use it for all sorts of things – cooking, cleaning, going to the loo, and it's easy to take it for granted. But once you have no running water (something that once happened to me for three whole days) you begin to understand how much you rely on it. So let me quickly explain how water gets into your house, and what you can do when things go wrong.

Water comes from water mains that run under the road and into your house. Then a service pipe runs to the water company's stopcock (stop laughing, this is serious), which is essentially a big tap. Everything up to this point is the responsibility of the water supplier, but after this it's down to you, so it's a good idea to know some basics.

The main pipe bringing the water in is often known as the rising main, and in most houses this and the stopcock can be found below or near the kitchen sink. The cold tap is always a direct offshoot from the main supply, so that the water is OK to drink.

HOW TO AVOID WATER PROBLEMS

- **Make sure your valves and stopcocks are working** – Find out where they are and make sure you can turn them off and on. Doing this once each uni year should be enough to make sure they don't seize up.
- **Check your washing machine pipes** – Washing clothes is important, so check the pipes because sometimes they can split or come loose. It's better to check these before something goes wrong. You really don't want to deal with it going to pot while you're running a washing cycle!
- **Avoid causing blockages** – In the kitchen, try not to wash bits of food, oil and fat down the drain, as these can block the sink.

Solving simple water problems

A lot of these problems sound like an ordeal to solve, but they're actually quite easy. It's better to fix them yourself if possible, rather than call your landlord out for a simple job.

UNBLOCKING A SINK

There are loads of really powerful and effective chemical products you can buy. Simply pour one down the plughole and see if it does the job.

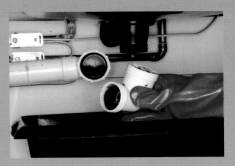

1 If it doesn't you'll need to use a more hands-on method. First, block the overflow (the little holey-bit halfway up the sink) with a cloth. This will create a vacuum, to start sucking at the gunk stuck down there. Then take a plunger, put it over the plughole and pump it up and down. This should move the blockage. Give it a good few tries before giving up. If plunging doesn't work then your problem might be deeper down.

4 If you still haven't found the problem you need to work further down the pipe. Unscrew the next section of the pipe so you can get at the main waste pipe.

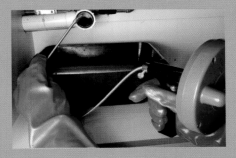

2 It's time to get under the sink. Put a bowl under the waste pipe coming down from the sink and unscrew the U-shaped plastic pipe. Clean out any gunk you find in there and put the pipe back. Remember not to use the tap above to clean it out – it's not a great idea, if you think about it.

3 Some sinks may have a 'bottle' trap, but even with this it's the same process as explained above.

5 Then use an auger (a nifty little gadget) to clear the blockage. Drag out around a metre from the auger and tighten the screw so it doesn't recoil. Force the coiled end into the pipe until you hit the blockage and dislodge it.

6 Put everything back as you found it, making sure you put any rubber washers back in place, and voilà! One freshly unblocked sink.

UNBLOCKING A TOILET

Considering the standard student diet of booze and greasy takeaways you can only imagine the evils involved in this little job. I'll keep it short and sweet and without too many gory details.

Again, try a chemical cleaner first, making sure you follow the instructions. If this fails, then use the auger (I really like that thing!) to unblock it in the same way as the sink. Make sure you seriously disinfect everything you've used afterwards, and wear rubber gloves throughout (yes, guys, it might not look very 'manly', but trust me, you don't want to get your hands in any of the stuff blocking the loo).

CISTERNS

Since you really want your toilet to flush, it's an idea to know how it works ...

When you press the handle, a lever in the tank pulls up the piston, forcing some water out through the siphon. This provides suction in the siphon, and the rest of the water follows, emptying the tank.

As the tank empties the float ball sinks to the bottom. This means that the float is no longer pressing against the valve, so water flows back into the tank, filling it up again. Clever, eh?

Common cistern problems are:

- **A dripping overflow pipe** – If the arm of your ballcock is metal you can bend it down gently so that the flow of water is stopped before it reaches the overflow level. If your arm is plastic, you can adjust it.
- **No water flow** – There might be a problem with the ball getting stuck on the edge of the cistern. To solve this, turn off the mains water, flush the loo

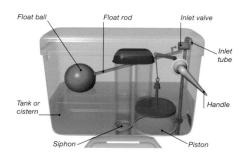

Float ball   *Float rod*   *Inlet valve*   *Inlet tube*   *Tank or cistern*   *Handle*   *Siphon*   *Piston*

and adjust the arm so that it doesn't catch on the cistern side at any height. Turn the water back on and check the cistern fills up properly before replacing the lid.

- **Crazy water flow** – If the water is more than going with the flow, gently raise the ball with your hand. If the flow continues you need to replace (or maybe repair) the valve.
- **The loo is having a moan** – If your toilet is making a grumbling sound, your cistern valve either needs dismantling, cleaning out (because of a build-up of stuff or limescale) or changing. Get a plumber to do this.

A SIMPLE FIX FOR A LEAKING VALVE

Sometimes all you need to fix a leaking valve is a new washer. Modern valves tend to use a diaphragm washer. Repair kits are also available for the older types of valve. You can get these from all good hardware stores.

It's well worth fixing this yourself. We once had this problem in one of the flats I lived in, and not knowing what to do we called an emergency plumber. With the call-out cost and his quick response we got stung for just over £80, for a job that should have cost a few quid and five to ten minutes' work! DIY really can save you wads and wads of cash.

Light

OK, so this bit isn't just about light, but electricity in general. It's another thing that you seriously take for granted until you find yourself sitting in the dark with no light, no computer and no television, and have to try and navigate around the place using the flashlight app on your phone!

Electricity is dangerous stuff – it can quite literally kill you – so there are only a few things you're allowed to do yourself. You can change plugs, plug sockets and light switches and fittings, as long as you aren't doing it in a kitchen or bathroom – water and electricity don't get along, so throw some students into the mix and you're looking at potential disaster!

WHEN THE LIGHTS GO OUT

This is going to sound a little patronising, but you'd be surprised how many people don't know this.

■ If the lights and power go off, first check that it's just your house that's got no lights – if the rest of the street is basked in light then it's your problem, and not a power-cut. In this case it is more than likely a fuse has gone. It's a simple fix.

■ Go to your fuse box (it's best to learn where this is when you move in), and look for the one switch that's pointing in a different direction to the rest. Flip it back up the right way and you should have light. A variety of things could have caused this – most likely a lightbulb that has blown or a dodgy hairdryer or kettle. Find and fix (or bin) the culprit to avoid it happening again.

REPLACING A PLUG

Most modern plugs are sealed units but if you have an appliance without a plug or one with an old-style plug, here's how to change it.

1 Start by unscrewing and removing the plug cover.

2 Then unscrew one side of the flex clamp while just loosening the other side.

3 Unscrew the three small wires from the pins.

4 Twist the metal strands at the end of the wires and place into the appropriate fixing hole in the new plug. Double check that they are all secured in place properly.

5 Make sure you are using the correct fuse for the appliance the plug is for.

6 Fasten the flex under the clamp and screw the plug cover back on.

SHELVES

Putting up some adjustable shelves is a quick-fix solution to gain extra space. Make sure you check it's OK with your landlord first.

ADJUSTABLE SHELVES

These are a great invention as you can change the height of the shelves to suit your purposes – and if you decide at a later stage to put tall books in a different place, you can just move the brackets and shelf to suit.

1 Make sure the supports will be about 10cm in from the end of the shelf. Hold the support against the wall and mark the top fixing point through the hole.

4 Now get the next vertical support and hold it in place, using your spirit level across the top to ensure they line up – be careful which way up the support is, as sometimes they are different from top to bottom. Make sure the second one is the same way around as the first. Repeat the same procedure as before for fixing the support in place.

2 Drill the hole (once you've checked for wires and pipes), push the correct wall plugs into the holes, and screw the support into place.

5 Put the brackets into the supports at the height you want them, starting with the top shelf. Make sure both brackets are the same number of slots down from the top so that the shelf will be level.

6 Place the wooden shelf into place on the brackets and check the overhang is equal either end. Use your bradawl to make pilot holes on the bottom of the shelf through the supports. Again, start with the top, as there's then space to work.

3 Use a spirit level to check the support is straight and continue to mark the remaining holes. Push the support to the side and drill and plug the holes.

7 Remove the shelf and drill small pilot holes, being careful not to drill right through the shelf (put some tape around the drill bit to mark the correct depth to be on the safe side). Put the shelf back into position and screw it to the brackets.

Living in a shared house

You think you're moving in with your best buddies, but it's a well known saying that you don't really know someone until you've lived with them. It can take mere weeks to go from smiling, happy best mates to hated, sworn enemies – over things as trivial as whose turn it is to do the washing-up.

Living in a house-share takes just a little bit of understanding and give-and-take to keep things running smoothly.

Split the bills, split the grief

Everyone hates paying bills – FACT! Sadly, there will be a few of them to pay in your house, and once you sign your tenancy agreement, you're all responsible for making sure they are paid. Don't put the entire burden of paying the bills on one person; take on the responsibility for one each if possible. This shares out the stress of paying and also gives any one of you a bit more leverage if someone is being a bit late in paying their share – they are more

likely to pay you if they need you to pay your share of their designated bill.

To avoid the usual feuds and potential murders caused by household financial issues, chat about the house finances every now and again to make sure everything is in order. It is easier to keep track with one of the bill-splitting apps you can get on your phone, such as Splitwise.

Be considerate

Just because you think it's a good idea to have an impromptu party at 3:00am on Tuesday morning doesn't mean that your

housemates will agree with you! They might have an early lecture or need to concentrate on an important essay. Basically, try to consider the other people you live with. Keep your music to a reasonable volume at night, don't trash the place and leave it that way, etc. Thinking about what the people you live with want can help keep everything harmonious and will result in everyone being in a much better mood. Then it's a good time to have a party!

Cleaning

ROTAS ARE GOOD

It would be nice to think that everyone will simply pitch in with their fair share of the cleaning, but this almost never happens in a student house. So draw up a rota, equally sharing out the jobs that need doing each week. The job can then be ticked off when it's done and you can see who's doing what. Of course, everyone should at least clean up the mess they've made themselves. Check out the cleaning list that follows to see what needs doing.

WHAT NEEDS TO BE DONE
Bathroom
With all the bodily stuff that goes on in the bathroom it's safe to say this is a place that's really best kept clean!

- Clean your toilet once a week. Nobody likes doing this job but it's essential. Wipe down the seat (and under it), give the bowl a good scrub with a toilet brush and squirt some toilet-cleaning product under the rim (then wash it all away after a short period). This can take just a few minutes and can make a world of difference. Keep a separate cloth by the toilet (i.e. don't use the same one on the sink!)
- Wipe down sinks and taps once a week.
- Same thing with showers and baths – all sorts of gunk can gather in these places. If you're standing in a pool in the shower, it means you need to clear out the rubbish (mainly hair) gathering in the plughole. Modern fittings will be removable (if not – call your landlord).
- Shower curtains should be washed once a month.
- In a house-share with lots of people liquid soap is more hygienic than a bar of soap, which can be a place for germs to build up.
- Avoid sharing towels and facecloths – they're a very quick way to share lovely infections and germs with each other.
- Clean floors once every few weeks.

Kitchen

You prepare and eat food in the kitchen, meaning you need to keep it clean and germ-free. Remember what you do in this room has a high chance of ending up in your mouth, and no one wants dirt and germs in there, do they?

- Regularly wipe down surfaces, cookers, hobs etc with disinfectant cleaning products.
- Don't leave pots to fester. It will get to the point where no one will take responsibility for the mouldy Everest of dirty pots and pans in the sink – but someone needs to do it.
- Empty and clean your fridge regularly. See the section on healthy eating on page 65 for tips on when to chuck food away.
- Don't use the same towel for drying pots and hands.
- Don't use the same cloth for wiping surfaces and washing the pots.
- Regularly replace the sponge you use to wash the pots.
- Clean floors once every few weeks.
- Empty the bins regularly, preferably before the rubbish is spilling out all over the floor and the whole room smells like a tip.

Bedroom

You spend about a third of your life asleep, and what with the other main activity that goes on in the bedroom … you really need this place not to be a grotty hell-hole. If it is, trust me, none of the aforementioned activity is likely to take place.

- Empty the bins regularly.
- Dust and wipe surfaces weekly.
- Hoover the floors weekly, especially if you have carpets. This can be a place for dust and dirt to build up. Hoovering for the first time in new student digs you might be surprised to find that the carpet is actually red rather than the off-grey colour you thought it was!
- Now, this is the biggie in the bedroom – change your sheets weekly (you can, maybe, get away with every two weeks). If you don't, you really don't want to find out what kind of creepy crawlies and germs are building up right where you sleep. You sweat all night (even more so in summer), and you wouldn't wear the same sweaty clothes for weeks on end, would you? Wash sheets, duvet covers and pillowcases on a high temperature wash to kill off all the little nasties. Nice clean sheets also feel amazing!

The whole house

Make sure the basic cleaning points listed above are done throughout the whole house. It might all seem like a lot of hard work, but none of this is particularly time-consuming and it can make a whole heap of difference in helping to keep you clean and healthy.

Chapter 4
Healthy body, fit mind

Taking responsibility for yourself at university also means looking after the health of your body and mind. It's important to stay healthy, in shape and well enough to complete your degree. Plus, if you're an overweight, badly groomed, smelly mess you're not likely to be very attractive to anyone.

Basic health and hygiene

We all know the stereotypes. Students are unhygienic, they barely wash, and many don't wash their clothes that often. It's a bit harsh to agree, but in the case of some people I've encountered this isn't so far from the truth. The stereotypes have to originate from somewhere!

Now, you don't need to be a clean freak, washing everything down with disinfectant several times a day to keep germs at bay, but there's a basic level of hygiene that's essential to keeping you healthy and giving you a fighting chance against all the illnesses floating around.

Personal hygiene

Nobody wants to be the smelly person in lectures! There may be a reason no one's sitting next to you.

Personal hygiene basically refers to the cleaning and grooming of your body. This is going to sound a little bit patronising, but trust me, some people really do ignore these very basic hygiene essentials.

- **Shower (or bathe) regularly** – Once a day would be preferable, but you could get away with it for a couple of days. Any more than that and you'll be getting a bit smelly.
- **Wash your face and neck daily** – These are exposed all the time to dirt and other cack. It'll make you look better and make you feel fresh.
- **Clean your teeth twice a day** – As well as keeping your gob healthy (helping to keep your teeth in your mouth), it helps keep your breath fresh. Bad breath is a terrible thing, especially if you're talking to that hottie from your seminar group. And don't just brush your teeth – floss regularly to get rid of the gunk between them, and finish off with some nice mouthwash. After all that you'll have lovely fresh breath.
- **Wash your hair a couple of times a week** – Think about it. Your head sweats a lot and what soaks up all that sweat and odour? Yes, that's right – your hair. Smelly hair is pretty horrible and it's not a hard thing to sort out. Give it a wash, you'll feel better for it.

We all know the stereotypes. Students are unhygienic, they barely wash, and many don't wash their clothes that often.

- **Wash your clothes regularly** – You know all that sweat coming from your body during the day? Well, that builds up on your clothes, so even if you're washing your body regularly your clothes can still pong. With most smelly folk it's their clothes causing the stink, and not so much their body.

Washing your clothes

It might not be something you've ever really thought about before, what with your old laundry fairy (or 'mother') taking your dirty clothes away and then returning them all clean and ironed, but now you have to wash your own clothes. If you don't you'll stink, simple as that!

Follow this basic guide on how to conquer the dreaded washing machine so that your clothes come out clean and the same size as they went in.

How to wash your clothes

The first time you come to use a washing machine it's probably going to seem like some highly complicated piece of machinery designed to baffle and bemuse you. Modern washing machines come with a fine array of settings, but let me keep it pretty simple for you so that you can at least get started:

1 **Separate your white clothes from your coloured clothes** – This will avoid all your whites coming out pink because of some rogue red sock.
2 **Open the door** – That's the big, usually round, thing in the middle with a glass front.
3 **Stick your dirty washing in the hole inside**.
4 **Close the door**.
5 **Open the drawer at the top** (usually in the right or left corner).
6 **Add your detergent and fabric softener** – The different slots usually confuse people. Put the detergent in the biggest slot, and the fabric softener in the smallest slot. (Read the instructions on the detergent as some go straight in with the clothes.)
7 **Turn the dial** (or press the

buttons) to select whichever setting you require – the details of the different settings will be on the front of the machine. Washing at 30° should be sufficient and will save you energy.
8 **Sit and wait**.
9 **Take out the clothes, shake well and hang them up to dry**.
10 **Iron your clothes**, if necessary.

Washing clothes – some frequently asked questions

HOW MUCH WASHING SHOULD I PUT IN THE WASHING MACHINE?

The answer to this might be a bit confusing. The thing is, you really don't want to overfill or underfill your washing machine. Overfilling can cause the clothes to move round the washing machine drum in one huge mass, which means that the clothes won't wash properly – in addition it can damage the machine. It might also not clean all the detergent off your clothes, which could cause a nasty shock for your skin when you put your pants on!

But you do need to at least fill the drum to get the most economical use from the machine and to save you cash from doing loads of unnecessary washing. Also under-loading means that your clothes can build up on

THOSE LAUNDRY CODES

While we're on the subject of washing machines – if you want to avoid shrinking or changing the colour of your clothes, check these symbols on the labels before you wash, iron or tumble dry them.

The wash tub indicates the most appropriate programme for that particular fabric.

The maximum temperature is shown in °C. These will be 95, 60, 50, 40 or 30°C. In addition to the temperature a bar may be present below the wash tub symbol.

Where there is no bar below the wash tub maximum agitation is recommended. This symbol appears on robust fabrics such as cotton and linen.

Where a single bar is shown beneath the wash tub, the washing action (agitation) should be reduced. This symbol is found on more delicate fabrics such as poly cotton, acrylics and viscose.

A broken or double bar beneath the wash tub symbol shows that only the most gentle wash action is required, as the fabric is likely to contain washable wool or silk.

The wash tub symbol with a cross through it means that the fabric is not suitable for washing.

Where a hand is shown in the wash tub, the garment may be hand washed but should not be machine washed.

Chlorine bleach may be used.

Do not use chlorine bleach.

The letter within the circle advises the dry cleaner which type of solvent can be used.

A circle with a cross means that the garment is unsuitable for dry-cleaning.

*One dot = Cool
Two dots = Warm
Three dots = Hot*

Cross = Do not iron

The information shown in the square gives the recommended drying method for that fabric.

Today many fabrics can be tumble-dried and this is indicated by a circle within the square. The most suitable heat setting for the garment is indicated by the addition of 'dots' within the circle.

One dot indicates low or half heat is required – normally synthetic fabrics.

Two dots indicates high or full heat is required – normally cotton fabrics.

A cross within the circle, or across the square indicates that the garment should not be tumbledried.

just one side of the drum. This can again damage the machine, because the load is out of balance and can cause violent banging when the drum spins. Breaking the washing machine isn't a good idea because then you'll either have to visit the laundrette or have increasingly smelly clothes until it's fixed.

So, fill the drum, pat the clothes down lightly, and make sure there's a reasonable gap between the top of the clothes and the top of the drum. A 3in or 4in gap should be enough – that's roughly the width of your hand.

WHY AREN'T MY CLOTHES COMING OUT CLEAN?

So you've done everything mentioned above but your clothes still aren't what you'd call clean. There are several things that could be causing this:

- You're using low-quality detergent.
- You're using the wrong programme on the machine.
- You've overloaded the machine.
- You're not using enough detergent (especially in hard-water areas).
- You've used the 'half load' button for a full load, meaning that the clothes haven't been rinsed properly.
- There's a blockage in the pumping system, meaning that water isn't being pumped out properly, which again is causing poor rinsing.
- The drum is broken and not spinning properly.

Ironing

It's a dull but necessary chore – unless, that is, you want to look all creased and scruffy, or you are super-organised with your washing and drying.

Obviously you need to make sure that there's water in the iron (that's where the steam comes from that gets rid of the creases), and that it's plugged in and switched on (this is what generates the heat that makes the steam that gets rid of the creases ...). Make sure you have an ironing board set up. Don't try ironing on the bed or floor – bad things can happen.

How to iron shirts

- Start on the collar. Stretch it over the end flat bit of the ironing board and run the hot iron over it a few times till it's all flat and crease-free. Turn it over and do the other side.
- Next the sleeves. It's best to iron the back of the sleeves first and then the front. Stretch the larger part of the sleeves across the flat bit of the ironing board, and iron the whole of one side of each sleeve before moving to the other side. Iron towards the cuffs and then iron the cuffs last.
- Now for the rest of the shirt. Stretch it as flat as you can over the ironing board. Iron from one side to the other, slowly smoothing out the creases as you go.
- Hang the shirt up as soon as you've finished – otherwise it will get creased all over again.

How to iron dresses and skirts

- Start by stretching the skirt section of the dress over the point at the end of the ironing board. If you have to deal with pleats, start at the bottom and work towards the top. Flat surfaces are much easier to deal with. Work round the skirt with fast strokes.
- If you can't get the skirt over the point just stretch it as flat as possible over the board and start from the back and work forward. Do both sides. Again, hang it up when finished.

How to iron trousers

- Turn the trousers inside out and begin with the top. Iron round the waistband and move towards the pockets. Iron both sides of the pockets. Iron along the seams. Do it all with smooth, quick strokes of the iron.
- Turn the trousers back round the right way and use the iron to press the creases out of the front part.
- Place the trousers with the legs parallel to the board and iron each leg, making sure all the creases are gone on both sides.
- Then hang them up right away to make sure you haven't wasted your time!

How to do without an iron

Lots of modern hi-tech material is non-creasing and doesn't need ironing – all sports wear, for example. And it is possible to get through life without any ironing at all. You just have to be there when your wash finishes, get it out of the machine straight away, shake vigorously and hang it up to dry on clothes hangers.

What you need to eat

All the nagging about healthy eating gets a bit boring, doesn't it? Why can't you just eat what you like? The simple answer is that you can! What you shove down your throat is up to you entirely, but there's a reason people bang on about healthy eating – it will have loads of benefits for you in both the short and the long term.

A better diet will give you more energy, and less chance of becoming ill. But healthy eating doesn't mean giving up on your favourite foods (although a greasy kebab every night really isn't recommended), or mean you need to spend hours slaving in the kitchen. It's all about balance, and it can be easy to keep on top of a decent diet. Try to see things like chocolates and takeaways as treats rather than part of your normal eating habits.

Here's a basic list of what you should be sticking in your body each day:

- **Starchy carbohydrates** – 5–8 portions.
- **Fruit** – At least 3 portions per day (but more would be good).
- **Vegetables** – A least 3 portions per day (but more would be good).
- **Dairy foods** – 3 portions.
- **Protein foods** – 2–3 portions.
- **Fatty and sugary foods** – 1 per day maximum – try to do without if possible!

Now that gives you loads of choice, doesn't it? There's really nothing wrong with that list. In case you have no idea what foods go into these categories (fruit and vegetables are fairly straightforward so don't need explaining), try these suggestions to get you going:

STARCHY CARBOHYDRATES
- Wholemeal bread.
- Potatoes.
- Wholemeal pasta.
- Brown rice.
- Oat-based cereal such as granola.

PROTEIN
- Meat.
- Fish.
- Shellfish.
- Eggs.
- Beans and other pulses.
- Nuts or seeds.
- Tofu.

DAIRY
Dairy products are amazing sources of protein but they need their own category here. Don't go for low-fat, they often have the goodness removed and sugar added.
- Whole or semi-skimmed milk.
- Plain natural, or Greek yoghurt.
- Soft or cottage cheese.
- All types of hard cheese.

If you're intolerant to dairy or a vegan, give calcium-enriched soya dairy products a go.

SUGARY FOODS
You really need to try and keep these to a minimum. There are large quantities of sugar in processed foods, so cut it out where you can. Don't add sugar to tea and coffee and keep your recommended intake to things you just can't do without – you know what you really crave, like chocolate (everyone loves chocolate) or biscuits. It's not like you can't indulge your taste-buds every once in a while, just try and keep your diet to the healthy foods above.

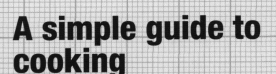

A simple guide to cooking

When it comes to food most students fall into one of three categories.

The first is experienced, independent and self-sufficient, even upon arrival on their first day. They've most likely just returned from their gap year and you're never quite sure how they learned everything they know. Their cupboards are full of exotic spices, which you're told you can only get from a guy he knows in a small market stall in a hidden Asian backwater. He raves about brown rice, green tea and soy and always has the necessary natural cure for any given problem.

The second group consists of those who are inexperienced and lazy. You rarely see these guys in the kitchen. Their cupboard holds just a bottle of ketchup and a solitary, grubby spoon. You suspect they have a deal with the local pizza company to deliver through the ground floor window so that they don't need to get dressed to answer the door, and the only way you're sure they're still alive is by the decimated remains of takeaway packaging that fills the communal bin in the kitchen the day after it gets emptied.

Most people fall into the third and final group, which is the complete newbies. Cooking isn't something they'll have ever had to think about before, and now they've been thrown in at the deep end to feed themselves and, hopefully, learn how to eat healthily.

Cooking is an important life skill and the techniques that you learn during uni will stick with you for the rest of your life. In short, it's well worth learning the basics and developing some good habits now, as these will serve you well in years to come.

Bearing in mind how important a healthy diet is for your physical and mental health, it seems sensible to provide a few basic food and cooking tips to help get you started:

Kitchen essentials

Stocking your cupboard for the first time can be a little pricey. Some things are worth the investment and some are more of a luxury, but all of them are useful tools to have at your disposal. Firstly check what's provided in your halls or student house (the previous tenants may have left everything you need).

UTENSILS

- **A large frying pan** – Generally used for cooking meat but also good for late-night drunken slapstick comedy re-enactments.
- **A medium saucepan** – For pasta, rice and sauces. If you can afford it, it's good to have a small saucepan as well, because it's more efficient for cooking things like eggs and gravy.
- **A small, sharp chef's knife** – The quality of knives can vary so much. Again, if you can afford a

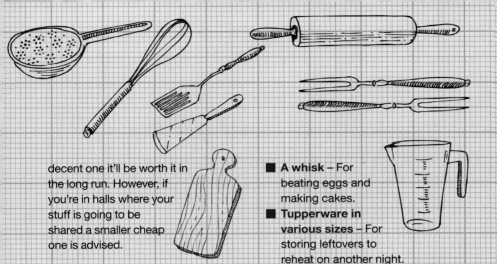

decent one it'll be worth it in the long run. However, if you're in halls where your stuff is going to be shared a smaller cheap one is advised.

Also necessary are:

- A spatula.
- Two wooden spoons.
- A cheese grater.
- A can opener.
- A bottle opener.
- Oven gloves.
- A sieve.
- A chopping board.
- Most people also recommend a dedicated chopping board just for meat, to avoid any risk of contamination.

The remaining items are less vital but will come in useful. You can pick them up cheap from charity shops, on eBay, or perhaps even persuade your parents to donate them:

- **A toaster** – Many students try to live on toast alone!
- **A kettle** – For boiling up a cup-a-soup and those endless cups of tea.
- **A wok** – For communal stir-fry night. Also good for all sorts of quick and easy meals.
- **A measuring jug** – For measuring stuff!

- **A whisk** – For beating eggs and making cakes.
- **Tupperware in various sizes** – For storing leftovers to reheat on another night.

CUPBOARD STUFF
- Washing-up liquid.
- Salt and pepper.
- Olive oil.
- Soy sauce.
- Dried pasta/spaghetti.

And, of course, you'll need loads of plates, cutlery, glasses and mugs. I'd suggest at least two of everything, because they tend to go missing when flat mates 'borrow' them and there'll never be a clean set when you want them.

Once you have all the stuff sorted in your kitchen you're going to need to know how to use it to make food. Some of this advice might seem a little basic and patronising, but seriously, some of this stuff seems hard until you know what you're doing. Here are a few cooking basics and some classic easy recipes in order to get you started.

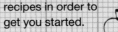

How to chop an onion

It's a real kitchen basic, but often done wrong and sometimes dangerously so.

The first common mistake is to cut the onion towards your fingers, but there's a much more effective method to slice an onion and keep your digits.

1 First, chop off both ends and slice across the middle (in the direction of the grain, rather than across it). Peel the skin off. You should now have two half spheres with flat ends.

2 Place one half on its flat edge with the flat ends to the left and right. Holding the onion with your left hand (assuming you're right-handed) chop straight down about half a centimetre in from the right. Continue this action by moving further to the left until you get to the other end.

3 Then take about half the strips you'll have now cut and turn them sideways so that you have a little semicircle-shaped stack. Then repeat the action of chopping down as before, from right to left. You'll see that this leaves you with small cubes, utilising the existing layers of the onion. If you wish you can then dice these further by creating a small pile of the cubes on the board and then, gripping towards the tip of the knife (but keeping your fingers well clear of the blade!), rocking the knife back and forth, like a seesaw, across the pile.

How to boil an egg

Delia Smith always answers the question 'How do you boil an egg?' with 'Carefully.' She has a very valid point. It isn't tricky, but it's certainly worth taking care to get it just right.

SOFT-BOIL METHOD

Boil just enough water to cover the egg in a small pan. Add a pinch of salt and lower in the egg with a spoon. If the egg has just come out of the fridge you should prick the rounded end with a pin to avoid it cracking when you place it in the water.

At this point it's important to ask whoever's having breakfast with you, 'How would you like your eggs?' It might seem like a strange question but everyone has a different preference, and knowing what it is is important in helping you gauge the next step: the timing.

Simmer for one minute, then remove from the heat, place the lid on the pan and leave for six to seven minutes (the longer you leave it the firmer and creamier the yolk will be).

HARD-BOIL METHOD

Add the egg to cold water in the pan then bring the heat to a simmer. Put on a timer for six minutes (seven for the yolk to be cooked through). Then comes the most important bit. Upon removing the egg, douse it in cold water until it's cool enough to handle. You can now carefully peel the egg and serve.

How to make an omelette

First, break some eggs into a bowl (two to three eggs per person), season with a little salt and pepper and then mix with a fork. Then add 40g of grated cheese. Add some oil or butter to a medium-sized pan and bring it to a very high heat.

When the butter is bubbling you may add the eggs, making sure they're evenly spread across the pan. Follow this by gently pulling the edges towards the centre with a spoon as you tilt the pan back and forth. The uncooked egg will flow into the gaps that you create.

After about 30 seconds of this simply fold the omelette in half and dish it up. It will go on cooking for a little even on the plate, so allow it to rest for a minute before eating.

How to make poached eggs

Don't bother with those poaching cups – just boil some water in a large pan, add a splosh of vinegar, crack your egg into a cup and gently tip it into the water. Let it cook for approx. 3–4 minutes. Use a slotted spoon to lift it out. The only thing you should watch out for is how fresh your eggs are. If they've been on a supermarket shelf for a while, then they'll spread out in the water. If you've got some lovely fresh free-range eggs they'll stay tight. Serve on mashed avocado on toast.

How to cook pasta

Pasta is a big part of most students' staple diet. It's cheap and filling and there are a lot of variations you can play with to keep it interesting.

Boil plenty of water (enough to generously cover your pasta) and add a pinch of salt. I'd recommend 85g of pasta per person as a sensible amount. Add this pasta and give it a quick stir to make sure it's all separated. If you're cooking spaghetti, drop it in the middle of the pan so that it splays out against the edges and gently press the tops until you feel it start to bend down into the water.

Allow the pasta to boil for a further 9–12 minutes (depending on the cooking instructions and your personal taste).

Drain the pasta in a colander – but not too thoroughly, as a little water helps bond the sauce to the pasta. Do not add oil, as this doesn't allow the sauce to stick to the pasta and it won't absorb any flavour! Some chefs suggest keeping a small cup of the water the pasta was cooked in to add to the sauce; again this allows the sauce to mix nicely with the pasta.

How to cook rice

To cook rice well you need a pan with a lid, or a cast iron pot.

Measure out your rice (approx. 65ml per person), measure it in a cup so that you can see how much volume the rice is. Heat the pan, with some oil or a knob of butter, and then add the rice. Turn over gently so the rice is consistently coated in the oil or melted butter. Then use the mug you placed the rice in to measure out the same amount of water, plus a little splash more. Stir in a good pinch of salt. Bring slowly to the boil, then place the lid on the pan and turn the heat right down to the lowest setting. Simmer for 10 minutes for white rice and 40 minutes for brown rice. Remove the lid, put a tea towel over the pan and leave it to rest off the heat for a further ten minutes. This allows the grains to absorb the steam and creates a lovely fluffy texture, fork through and serve.

Baked potatoes

The key to a great jacket potato is that beautiful crisp, crunchy skin with a soft, fluffy interior. To start, prick your potato with a fork a couple of times, or use a sharp knife to create two slits as a cross on the top. If you like a soft skin, add a thin coating of olive oil all over. If you prefer a crisp skin, leave it as it is. Put your potatoes in the centre of the oven at a mid to high heat for between one and two hours. For a fluffy interior, as soon as you remove them from the oven, bash the top so the slits split. This allows the steam to escape. Add plenty of butter, salt and black pepper. So many things work well as an additional filling – a few things you could try include grated cheese, sour cream, baked beans, chilli, and tuna mayo. If you're feeling like something a bit different you could try baking a sweet potato.

How to cook steak

The secret to a good steak is a little patience. To start, heat a frying pan but don't put any oil in it. To lock in the flavour and juices, season the steak on a chopping board and coat it in olive oil. Then place it in the pan and leave it. Just wait until the colour rises through the meat until you can see it's reached about halfway up the side. Then flip it and wait again. It's very tempting to want to jiggle the pan and check how the undersides are doing, but it's best not to. After you've seared both sides in this way, turn down the heat and flip another two times to allow the centre to cook through (assuming you want a medium rare steak). The less rotations the better as it will only allow more juice to escape. If you prefer a rarer steak allow a shorter time between the first two flips.

THE SIMPLEST SAUCE IN THE WORLD

This works well with pretty much anything. You can add it to pasta or rice or use it as a steak sauce.

Gently heat some double cream in a frying pan, crumble in a stock cube and mix until it's a consistent colour. That's it. Add it over some pasta and chicken to create a Carbonara or add some peppercorns and serve it over a delicious lump of steak.

Easy chilli con carne

You don't need to be that accurate with the ingredients!

SERVES 4

1 onion (chopped)
1 green or red pepper (chopped)
1 large can chopped tomatoes
1 clove of garlic (optional)
1 tablespoon tomato puree
1 tablespoon oil
3 teaspoon chilli powder (or to taste)
1 beef stock cube, crumbled
500g /1lb beef mince
1 large tin red kidney beans (or large tin chilli beans)
salt and black pepper
Fresh coriander, to serve (optional)

- Peel and chop the onion and pepper.
- In a large pan heat the oil and cook the onion and pepper until softened.
- Crush or finely chop the garlic and add to the pan. Cook for another two minutes.

- Add the meat and cook until browned, stirring to break up the lumps. Spoon any excess fat into a bowl.
- Add the chilli powder and seasoning.
- Add the tomatoes, puree, chilli powder, a tin full of water, and the stock cube. Mix well.
- Cook for at least 45 minutes to an hour, stirring occasionally. Add the kidney beans, check for seasoning, and cook for another 15 minutes.
- Serve with rice, or baked potato, or nachos. Freeze what you don't eat or keep it covered in the fridge for a couple of days.

Sweetcorn fritters

Good with bacon for breakfast, or serve with chicken or sausages. Also good for padding out a meal – makes it cheap! Serve drizzled with sriracha if you like a little heat.

110g/4oz self-raising flour
½ teaspoon of salt and black pepper
Pinch of nutmeg
2 beaten eggs
2 tablespoons of milk (full fat)
1 tin of sweetcorn (or the same amount of frozen sweetcorn defrosted in hot water)

Prepare batter mixture:
- Sift flour and seasonings.
- Whisk eggs and milk together and add to flour.
- Beat into a smooth batter with a wooden spoon.
- When you are ready to cook add the sweetcorn to the batter and stir it in.

Cook batter mixture:
- Heat a little oil in a frying pan.
- Cook spoonfuls of the mixture (like small flat pancakes) until puffed up and brown on each side – need to turn once.
- Keep warm in the oven until all of the mixture is cooked.

Big stew

Stew is the best and easiest meal to make. Add dumplings to make it tastier and cheaper – suet is cheaper than beef! You can stew any meat or even pulses if you are a veggie. What you choose to use as the liquid makes all the difference to the end taste. The following recipe gives one example that works but you could use:

Beef – red wine, beer, Guinness, tomatoes, beef stock, oxtail soup.

Chicken – white wine, chicken stock, condensed chicken soup, vegetable soup.

Lamb – red wine, minestrone soup, beef stock.

THICKENING

When the stew is nearly cooked you may need to thicken the sauce. If there is oil/fat on the surface spoon it off first. Mix a tablespoon of flour (plain flour or cornflour) to a smooth paste with cold water in a bowl. Spoon some of the hot sauce from the casserole into the bowl and mix. Tip the warm flour mix back into the casserole and stir (if you put the cold flour mix straight in, it will go lumpy). Put back into the oven for 20 minutes – add more if needed.

LEFTOVERS

You can reheat the stew again once (make sure it's gently cooked until piping hot throughout). Have it on pasta or rice. Put it in an ovenproof dish and cover with pastry for a pie or mashed potatoes.

Beef stew

SERVES 4

900g/2lb shin beef (stewing beef will do)
4 onions
2 tins tomatoes
4 cloves of garlic and some mixed herbs
Carrots or swede or mushrooms (or a mixture of all three)
Flour (about a couple of tablespoons)
Beef stock cube
Salt and pepper

- Season flour with salt and pepper.
- Chop meat into small cubes.
- Toss meat in seasoned flour.
- Fry meat in a little oil until it begins to brown and then transfer to a casserole dish.
- Add chopped onion and crushed garlic to the pan and fry for a few minutes – just to soften the onion.
- Add tinned tomatoes and herbs and heat.
- Add some Worcester sauce, a stock cube and salt and pepper. Transfer to casserole.
- Cook in a low oven (160°C) for at least 3 hours – better all day in a slow cooker.
- Add chopped carrot and mushrooms for last hour of cooking.
- Try adding red wine or beer for a change (fewer tomatoes).
- Add the dumplings to the top of the stew, and cook for another 20–30 minutes, uncovered, until they are golden on top.

DUMPLINGS

175g/6oz self-raising flour
75g/3oz beef suet
handful fresh parsley, chopped
salt

- Mix the ingredients together then slowly add enough cold water to make a soft dough.
- Roll into balls.
- Cook on top of the stew, or separately in a large pan of boiling water, until they float to the top, about 5–10 minutes. They should be risen and fluffy.

Pot-roast chicken

This is a great one-pot recipe which means it's quick to prepare and there's hardly any washing up. You can change around the vegetables depending on what you like (all root vegetables work well). You'll need to use a large casserole dish with a lid (or foil).

1 chicken (medium to small)
2 onions
2 leeks
2 carrots
2 sticks of celery
2 large potatoes
2 cloves of garlic
2 of any other vegetables you feel like adding
2 large glugs of white wine (optional)
2 large mugs of water
2 sprigs of thyme (or pinch of dried herbs)
2 bay leaves
2 teaspoons of salt (and a bit of pepper)

Put the chicken in the casserole. Peel and chop all the veg into large chunks and place around the chicken. Pour in the wine and water and sprinkle in the salt. Tuck in the thyme and bay leaves. Add some black pepper. Cover and put in the oven at 190°C. After 50 minutes take off the lid and give everything a good stir. Keep the lid off and put back in the oven for another 30 minutes.

Carve up the chicken and serve in big bowls with all the veg and delicious broth.

Pizza

It's best if you make your own dough but you can use a bought base, split, part-cooked baguettes, or even pitta breads. All quantities are approx – just add stuff until you get what you want!

TOMATO SAUCE

This sauce can also be used with pasta, and keeps in the fridge for a few days and freezes well.

1 onion, finely chopped
1 clove garlic, thinly sliced
2 tbsp virgin olive oil
1 tin tomatoes
salt and black pepper

Sweat the onion in the olive oil in a large pan until soft and translucent. Don't brown. Add the garlic and saute for a few more seconds, then pour in the tin of tomatoes. Swill the tin out with a dash of water and add to the pan. Cover, and cook on a slow simmer for about 10–15 minutes until the sauce is soft and thick. Add salt and pepper to taste. Leave to cool before using on a pizza, or your base will go soggy.

Toppings – thinly sliced peppers, mushrooms, onion, anchovies, bacon etc

- Spread the sauce thinly onto a dough base
- Top with one of the following combinations, or make up your own:
  Anchovies, tuna and olives
  Mushrooms and peppers
  Pepperoni and chillies
  Bacon and red onion
- Sprinkle with cheese; mozzarella, Cheddar and Parmesan all work well
- Bake in the oven at 220°C for approx 15 minutes for a raw base (or follow the instructions on the packet), but much less for baguette or pitta bread.

Pizza dough (for 6 bases)

If you need to take some frustration out on something – spend some time kneading a bit of pizza dough.

650g/1lb 5oz Italian 00 flour (strong white flour)
7g sachet of easy-blend yeast
2 teaspoons salt
25ml/1fl oz olive oil
50ml/2fl oz warm milk
325ml/11fl oz warm water

- Mix the flour, yeast and salt together in a large bowl and stir in the olive oil and milk. Slowly add the water, mixing well to make a soft dough.
- Put the dough on to a floured surface and knead for about five minutes, until smooth and elastic. Put it in a clean bowl and cover with a damp tea towel and leave

to rise for about 1½ hours, until doubled in size.

- Knead again until smooth and roll into a ball and wait for 30 minutes to 1 hour until it has risen again.
- Split the dough into six balls and roll them out on a floured surface until approx 20cm/8in in diameter.

Fruit crumble

The favourites are:

Berries Probably the easiest, as no prep is required, just buy a bag of frozen berries and tip them into the dish.

Apple Peel, core and slice cooking or eating apples. Add a sprinkle of cinnamon if you like.

Plum Remove the stones and cut into quarters.

Rhubarb Great with a bit of ground ginger.

All the above will need mixing with a couple of tablespoons of sugar. Cooking apples and rhubarb will need more.

IT'S A FRUIT FOOL

Stew some fruit (gooseberries or rhubarb are good) either in the microwave for 10 minutes or on a low heat on the hob for 15–20 minutes. When stewed (soft) mix in sugar until it's sweet enough for your taste. Stir in 200ml of custard (out of a carton or tin is fine). Whip up a small pot of double cream until stiff and fold in to the fruit mixture. Put into small bowls, glasses, or one large bowl and leave to cool, then chill in the fridge for 3–4 hours.

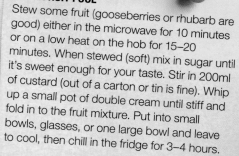

CRUMBLE TOPPING
4oz plain flour
2oz butter
2oz granulated sugar

- Rub the butter into the flour and sugar until it is like breadcrumbs.
- Spread on top of fruit and cook in an oven at 180 degrees until golden brown on top.
- Serve with custard, ice cream or cream.

The minimum-effort fitness plan

All the stuff associated with the typical student lifestyle – massive drinking sessions, staying in bed all day, takeaways – can take their toll on your body. And this is bad, not just for your chances of being attractive but also for the other important things at university, like studying! Unhealthy body, unhealthy mind.

The evidence is all there. Research from Tufts University in the US found that exercising at least three times a week left students with much better health and a lot happier than those who didn't. And the NHS say that everyone, whatever their age, should try and be active daily to stay physically and mentally healthy.

The thing is, it really isn't that hard to stay in shape. Based on NHS recommendations, here's the ultimate, minimum-effort student workout in two simple parts:

Part one

Set aside just 30 minutes, five days a week, for some exercise – this even gives you the weekend off. Half an hour? That's nothing, right? I mean, how long do you spend on social media – a lot more, I bet! You could even decide to walk or cycle everywhere, unless you live miles and miles from campus.

You need to be doing 'moderate-intensity aerobic activity' for these 30 minutes. Simply put, this is doing something that will raise your heart rate and make you sweat. Try these:

- Speed walking – this means fast, not dawdling please – or jogging.
- Cycling – great way to save bus fares.
- If you are already a keen runner or swimmer, you could run or swim for 15 minutes five days a week instead.

Easy – that's even less time. Done! That's it for part one – it really is as simple as that.

Part two

For another two or more days a week add some muscle-strengthening activities to the mix. You can do them on the same day as your aerobic activity or on your days off.

To get the real benefits of these activities you need to do them to the point where you struggle to do another repetition, and then keep building up till you can do more. Two or three sets will give you more benefits. Do these in sets of 12 repetitions.

Also make small changes to your daily routine. Reduce the amount of time you sit or lie down, take the stairs not the lift, walk a few extra stops instead of getting the bus – in fact avoid public transport altogether if you can walk or cycle the distance easily.

Choose an aerobic activity that fits easily into your daily routine and stick to a specific time of day when working out. Do it with a friend so you can motivate each other.

THE SIT-UP

While lying on your back with legs bent, feet together, knees together and fingertips on temples, sit up under control to a near vertical position so that the elbows can touch the tops of the knees. Ideally the feet should remain flat on the floor and the fingertips in touch with the temples. Don't be tempted to put the hands behind the head and pull up through the arms – this will injure the neck. Once vertical, open the arms to open the chest at the top position. Then lie back under control so that the head, shoulders and elbows are back in contact with the ground. Repeat the exercise, ensuring your form is correct.

SIT-UP PROGRESSIONS

- **Weight across chest** As for regular sit-up, but instead of placing fingers on the temples hold a weight placed on the chest under crossed arms. The abs have to work harder when sitting up.
- **Weight outstretched** As above but instead of holding the weight across the chest it's held in the air directly above the head. As the sit-up is performed the weight stays above the head, on the way up and the way down. It's important to keep it directly above the head and not allow it to come forward over the chest (which makes the exercise easier). This exercise has some effect on the shoulders depending on the weight held.
- **On fitball** As for normal sit-up, but instead of being done on the floor it's performed lying with the back on a fitball. Due to the instability of the ball

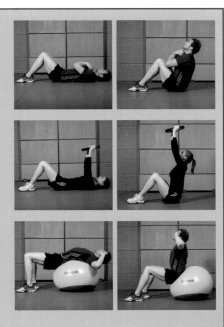

the general core muscles and abs have to work harder to exercise and remain balanced.

Keep your mind healthy

It's hard to believe that even a decade ago 'mental health' was not taken as seriously as it is now. Instead, many of its problems were ignored and talking about it was taboo, or a sign of weakness. 'Man up', or 'suck it up' or another dismissal is what you would likely hear. Thankfully, though, mental health issues are now being recognised as being as, if not more, important than physical ones, and it's better understood that they can lead to many physical problems as well.

This is good. Mental health is something that needs to be taken seriously. At its most damaging, issues with mental health has caused an epidemic in suicide, with 6,507 such deaths registered in 2018 according to the Office for National Statistics (ONS), equating to an average across males and females of 11 people in every 100,000. Of huge concern is the rise in suicide in people aged 10 to 24, and the highest rate of young female suicides ever recorded.

Despite this, it is still men who are more likely to commit suicide, with an average of 17 men in every 100,000 taking their own life. These statistics show the challenges we all face with mental health and how bad it can get.

It is therefore essential that we care for our minds as much as our bodies, know the signs of potential problems and ask for the right help when we need it. While each case, and person, is different, there are some common mental health problems you need to look out for.

UNI BLUES

University is a hard time for some of us, especially since it can be the first time that we have been on our own without the comfort and emotional safety nets of home and our families that we are used to.

Depression

We all feel down from time to time, whether from having a bad day or hearing some bad news, but depression is a different, very serious, often misunderstood matter.

First off, having depression doesn't necessarily mean that you are sad. The illness has many symptoms: for instance, you may feel apathetic, have no strong feelings towards anything and/or lose interest in things you used to enjoy.

Many things can trigger depression and its causes are not straightforward. Triggers can be things like bereavement, events in childhood, stress and relationship difficulties. But it is not just life experiences that can kick off depression – it can also be due to internal problems linked to hormone imbalance, sometimes due to changes in brain chemistry or blood sugar levels.

Below is a list of symptoms to look out. These are intended to help you spot whether or not there may be a problem. However, since self-diagnosis is never a good idea, if in doubt you should book an appointment to discuss this issue with your GP. If you feel reluctant, ask yourself this:

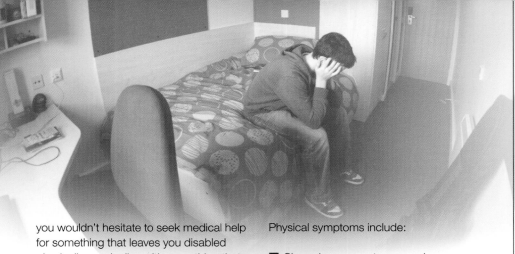

you wouldn't hesitate to seek medical help for something that leaves you disabled physically so why live with something that disables you mentally?

Psychological symptoms include:

- Continuous low mood or sadness that lasts around two or more weeks.
- Feelings of hopelessness and helplessness.
- Low self-esteem and loss of self-confidence. Feeling guilty, bad, unlikeable or not good enough and that life is too much to cope with.
- Reduced sex drive.
- Trouble concentrating and poor memory.
- Low mood in the morning and difficulty finding the will to get out of bed.
- Wanting to go to sleep and never wake up, having suicidal thoughts or wanting to harm yourself.
- Tearfulness.
- Feeling irritable and intolerant of others.
- Lack of motivation and little interest in things.
- Difficulty making decisions.
- Feeling empty inside.
- Feeling bored all the time.
- Increased feelings of anxiety.
- Can't see a future for yourself and thinking that everything is pointless.

Physical symptoms include:

- Slowed movement or speech.
- Change in appetite or weight (usually decreased, but sometimes increased).
- Constipation.
- Unexplained aches and pains.
- Lack of energy or lack of interest in sex.
- Changes to the menstrual cycle.
- Disturbed sleep patterns.

The good news is that depression is treatable – with counselling and medication – and just because you feel at your lowest point now doesn't mean it has to continue forever. There is no shame in feeling 'not normal' and you should openly discuss your issues with other people. If you do, you'll probably find that you are not the only person who feels this way. Just because

It's important that you get the help you need to deal with the problems of depression as soon as you can.

you are feeling certain things that are not openly talked about often does not make you 'mental' or 'weird'. Shutting yourself away from the world is not the answer, no matter how tempting it might feel sometimes; it will be detrimental to your social life and is bound to have a knock-on effect on your academic progress, which in turn is likely to fuel your depression.

So, I say it again: it is important that you get the help you need to deal with the problems of depression as soon as you can.

Stress

A common myth is that university is an easy three years, what with the mounds of spare time and unlimited lie-ins, and all that! And yet of course academic life is not at all stress-free, so it is essential that you learn to cope with stress in order that you can complete your studies and not make yourself ill.

It's also important to recognise that a certain level of stress is natural and helps you deal with the challenges you face every day: it improves your reaction times and heightens your senses, actually helping you to perform better! So, stressing a little before an exam or essay due date is a positive thing. But too much

stress is not, and can have serious effects on your life and health.

The initial signs of stress are:

- irritability
- insomnia
- loss of appetite
- headaches or dizziness

If you don't deal with stress it can lead to serious problems for your body and mind, such as:

- anxiety (feelings ranging from uneasiness to severe and paralysing panic)
- dry mouth
- churning stomach
- palpitations (pounding heart)
- sweating
- shortness of breath
- depression

If you experience any of these and they are affecting your life, book an appointment with your GP or find out what kind of counselling service your university offers. You can also help yourself further by taking regular exercise and eating a healthy diet, and avoiding excessive alcohol and all drugs.

WAYS TO DEAL WITH STRESS

- Talk to someone about what is worrying you.
- Do something that takes your mind off what is causing you stress.
- Plan work well so you have enough time to complete it in time.
- Eat healthily.
- Get enough sleep.
- Exercise and keep active.
- Limit the hours you work outside of your studies to help maintain a good work/life balance.
- If it all becomes too much, seek professional help.

Drugs and alcohol

Nights out, partying, pub crawls, pre-drinking and student life in general, all have an inevitable alcohol element, but young people are starting to realise this should just be part of their lives and not the dominating factor. The important thing when you're drinking or experimenting, is that you stay safe and in control.

Alcohol

Although there are more teetotal students about now, most will drink at uni, and some people will do it a lot. Because it's legal and everyone's doing it, alcohol isn't always treated with the same caution as other 'drugs'. Yes, it is a drug, admittedly a legal one but a drug all the same.

University will open up the world of drinking like never before – cheap booze at the union, and every bar in the city offering an array of drinks at ridiculous knockdown prices to lure you in through their door. There will be pressure for you to drink a lot, especially during Freshers' Week when it's seen as the 'normal' thing to do.

It's worth knowing what effect different types of booze will have on you. Check the label for the number of 'units' each drink has. Units measure the amount of alcohol you're drinking and help you compare the strength of different drinks.

THE HIGHS

It's obvious that being drunk is great fun. You're invincible, irresistible, the most interesting person ever with the best dance moves – or at least, you think you are, and perception is nine-tenths of the law (or something like that).

Booze is a nervous-system depressant, meaning your reactions

to just about everything will be slowed down and you'll feel everything less. It also exaggerates whatever mood you're in – so if you're happy you'll be happier, and if you're feeling sexy you'll feel sexier, etc. So it's best to leave the stuff alone if you're feeling a bit down...

In small amounts it reduces any anxiety and inhibitions you might have, making you feel more sociable and a 'better' person. It's like Popeye and spinach, but without the unnerving sudden muscle growth.

THE LOWS

With booze there's a fine line between that invincible feeling and ending up a slurring, unbalanced, vomiting mess. The more alcohol you drink the more your nervous system is suppressed and the less control you have over your body.

Of course, there's a chance that booze

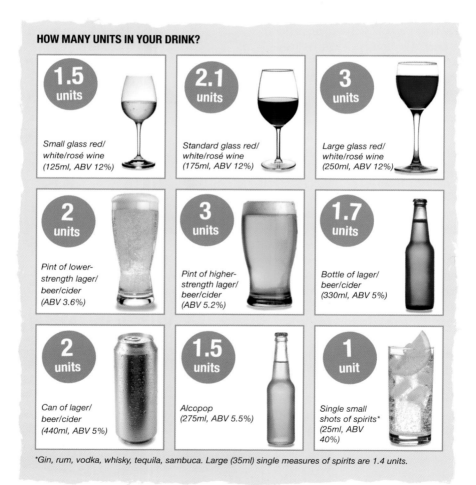

HOW MANY UNITS IN YOUR DRINK?

1.5 units
Small glass red/white/rosé wine
(125ml, ABV 12%)

2.1 units
Standard glass red/white/rosé wine
(175ml, ABV 12%)

3 units
Large glass red/white/rosé wine
(250ml, ABV 12%)

2 units
Pint of lower-strength lager/beer/cider
(ABV 3.6%)

3 units
Pint of higher-strength lager/beer/cider
(ABV 5.2%)

1.7 units
Bottle of lager/beer/cider
(330ml, ABV 5%)

2 units
Can of lager/beer/cider
(440ml, ABV 5%)

1.5 units
Alcopop
(275ml, ABV 5.5%)

1 unit
Single small shots of spirits*
(25ml, ABV 40%)

*Gin, rum, vodka, whisky, tequila, sambuca. Large (35ml) single measures of spirits are 1.4 units.

will make you more likeable, but there's an equal chance it'll turn you into someone people just don't want to be around. It can make you mouthy, argumentative and aggressive, and you'll have no way of controlling it. There's no way of knowing before you start drinking if you'll turn into a nice drunk or a nasty one.

Just because it's legal doesn't mean that alcohol doesn't have serious health problems. Excessive drinking can, and regularly does, lead to alcohol poisoning, which can lead to you being in a coma or even kill you. A lot of excessive use can cause such illnesses as liver damage, stomach cancer and heart disease.

On top of all these dangers, alcohol dependency (both physical and psychological) can take you by surprise. The more you drink the more you can drink, meaning you'll need to drink more and more just to get drunk. You may think you're brilliant because you can hold your drink when in reality you might be developing a drink problem!

Alcohol is a big killer. According to the Office of National Statistics there were 7,697 alcohol-specific deaths in 2017. That's around 12 people in every 100,000! And the number of these deaths has been growing in recent years, back up to the level they were in 2008 (when there was the highest number of deaths on record). With these stats in mind, it's worth watching what you do with booze so you don't become one of them.

The recommended alcohol limit that you shouldn't exceed is three to four units a day for men, and two to three units a day for women.

After a night (or day) of heavy drinking you shouldn't drink again for 48 hours, to allow your body to recover.

Drugs

We've all heard it: 'Say no to drugs,' 'Drugs are bad,' etc etc. Not the most helpful advice, is it? People take drugs – fact. At university people you know will take drugs, you might even pop the odd pill or smoke the odd spliff yourself. The key thing to know is what it'll do to you and how not to die doing it. Dying really does make things less enjoyable. Here are the common drugs you'll encounter on campus:

CANNABIS

Dope, weed, pot, hash, ganja, green – whatever you call it, cannabis is the most popular drug (other than booze) among students. And, while drug use in general is becoming less common among students, cannabis is still the most used drug both on and off campus; lots of  people still get 'stoned'. In fact, Home Office statistics for 2018 show that 7.2 per cent of adults aged 16 to 59 had smoked it in the previous year.

It comes in one of three forms: solid hash, bushy weed and oil, and can be smoked (with or without tobacco), eaten or drunk.

The highs

The effects are different from person to person. Some people become happy and relaxed and others take one puff and immediately feel sick. Other cannabis effects can be fits of giggles, becoming very hungry (known more commonly as 'the munchies'), wanting to talk a lot, hallucinations, a heightened awareness of senses and a feeling of time slowing down.

The effects of cannabis generally last from 30 minutes to eight hours, depending on the potency of the dose and method of ingestion.

The lows

How bad cannabis actually is has been a hot topic for debate for a long time, and isn't something we can go into here. You should know, though, that it is now a Class B drug again after a brief period as a Class C drug between 2004 and 2008, so do remember that it is illegal to possess or smoke it.

Using cannabis regularly has been associated with an increase in the risk of developing psychotic conditions and illnesses such as schizophrenia, although the precise effects of long-term cannabis use are not yet fully understood.

It's often been referred to as a 'gateway drug', leading to the use of harder drugs, but as the addictive quality of cannabis hasn't been confirmed many believe this fact to be as much due to the drug's illegality as to the drug itself.

Needless to say, as the drug takes over your body and mind you might end up doing or saying things you might regret later.

ECSTASY

The 'party drug' or the 'rave drug' – it's believed that E can change your life. It's a class A drug and can have as many destructive effects as other drugs that are seen as more serious.

A hallucinogenic amphetamine (that means it stimulates you and makes you see things), a pill is usually made up of a mixture of drugs, using synthetic drug

methylenedioxymethamphetamine (or MDMA, if that's too much of a mouthful). Pills are usually white and can vary in size.

It's not as popular as it used to be, with the British Crime Survey (BCS) reporting a drop in its use since the early 2000s, but this might be referring to just pills rather than E in all its forms. Some people think that the use of ecstasy powder is on the rise.

There has been an increase in people aged 16 to 24 taking Class A drugs over the past decade, with 2018/19 having the highest numbers since 2002/03 according to the Home Office. The number of people taking ecstasy contributes to this in a big way.

The highs

The effects vary wildly from pill to pill, as they contain different amounts of MDMA. Effects are quick to kick in, usually after around half an hour, and can last up to six hours, with a steady come-down afterwards.

Common effects of 'dropping an E' include strong feelings of affection and love towards friends (and people you've just met), empathy for people around you, and sounds, colours and emotions becoming much more intense.

There's no proof that ecstasy is an aphrodisiac, but many users claim that it is. It tends to make the experience more sensual rather than increasing the desire to have sex.

The lows

Ecstasy has some serious down sides. As your body begins to react with the drug you can experience bouts of nervousness, paranoia and uncertainty. 'Coming up', you'll feel your jaw tighten and heart-rate increase, along with potential nausea and sweating.

There's a serious danger of overheating and dehydrating as you dance all night in a hot sweaty club, and the feeling of invincibility the drug gives you will affect your ability to deal with these problems.

Mixing alcohol with ecstasy makes for a fatal cocktail. For some people ecstasy releases a hormone that stops them being able to pee, so this added to drinking too much alcohol can quickly interfere with the body's salt balance. This can be just as dangerous as not drinking enough water.

The 'come-down' really isn't that much fun – how does feeling tired, depressed and irritable for a longer period than the 'buzz' sound? Not great, I imagine. Plus everyone reacts to E differently, so you never know how dangerous it'll be for you – it's a real gamble. Users with heart conditions, asthma or epilepsy can have seriously bad reactions to E.

Figures quoted for the number of deaths caused by ecstasy vary, but it seems that they are at their highest for a decade. According to the ONS, there were eight deaths in 2010 and 57 in 2015. Figures published on Statista stated that this had risen to 92 in 2018. This is an alarming increase, with multiple causes. It's

clear, then, that you need to be careful to not become one of the growing numbers dying from taking ecstasy. And, like other drugs, it is of course illegal.

Regardless of which figures you want to believe, it's safe to say that taking ecstasy comes with a danger of death.

COCAINE

Use of cocaine is widespread – we see pictures of celebs snorting it, and rolled-up banknotes being passed around in club toilets happens a lot. According to ONS statistics cocaine use among 16–24-year-olds in the UK is at a nine-year high, with 6 per cent saying they had taken the drug in the previous year.

It can be snorted, injected or smoked. The most popular method is to snort it, so that it's absorbed directly into the bloodstream through the nasal tissues. You can also smoke a vaporised form of the drug or inject a liquid form straight into your bloodstream.

The highs

On cocaine you feel 'on top of the world' and have loads of energy. It raises your body temperature, suppresses hunger and makes your heart beat faster.

The different methods of taking cocaine take a varying amount of time to kick in, and the high lasts for different periods. You can get an immediate high from smoking it, with the high peaking at two minutes and lasting for around ten. Snorting takes a little longer to feel the effects, but the high lasts for around 20–30 minutes.

The lows

Coke is very, very addictive and makes chemical changes to your brain – so once you pop it it's pretty hard to stop.

The biggest danger is to your heart – the most important thing in your body. Cocaine will increase your blood pressure, heart rate and body temperature. Worse than all this, it constricts your blood vessels.

The combined effect of all this is that it's hard to get blood and oxygen round your body – something that you kind of need to happen in order to stay alive. Imagine trying to suck syrup through a straw instead of water!

This increases the risk of heart attacks and angina, and no matter what your age, when you're on cocaine there's a high risk of suffering from heart failure. This 'failure' can lead to coma or death.

This is worrying because cocaine is really dangerous. The 637 deaths from cocaine use accounted for a large proportion of the 16 per cent increase in deaths overall from drug poisoning in 2018/19, and was a massive increase from the 320 deaths in 2015. Clearly, more people are dying every year from this Class A drug. And that's before we even begin to talk about the cocaine industry and the murders and exploitation that spatter the supply chain… Just watch *Narcos* or any show about drug cartels – it'll put you off for life.

SPEED

Speed (amphetamine) does pretty much what it says on the tin – it makes you more awake, alert and hyperactive. It actually covers a range of amphetamines: amphetamine sulphate, dexedrine and dexamphetamine.

Usually sold in wraps as a powder, it's pink or brown to off-white in colour, all depending on what other stuff it's mixed with. 'Base' is much purer, pinkish-grey in colour and feels a bit like putty. Some amphetamines (like dexamphetamine) are available on prescription and usually come as little white pills.

Users rub speed on to their gums or snort it in the same way as cocaine. It's sometimes rolled up in a cigarette paper and swallowed (known as a 'speedbomb'). Some users mix it into drinks.

Speed is a Class B drug, but if it's prepared for injection it becomes a Class A drug.

The highs

It's all in the name 'speed' – it all gets very speedy. Speed gives you energy, makes you really confident and keeps you awake, which is why it's mostly used for going partying and clubbing.

The lows

Again, this drug really messes with your heart – something that really isn't good.

Speed causes a rise in heart rate and blood pressure, and causes your heart to race or beat erratically.

Regular use can cause significant health problems, as it reduces your need to eat and sleep. As well as your body, speed can also mess up your mind, causing paranoia, anxiety and a psychological dependency on it.

Another big problem is that you really don't know what you're getting when you buy speed. This is probably the least pure drug you can buy, with many samples containing less than 10% amphetamine, mixed with a variety of drug and non-drug powders – depending on the dealer this really can be anything, even washing powder or flour (both have been found in samples).

KETAMINE

Ketamine (or ket, or 'Special K') is powerful stuff with a short-acting hit. A powerful anaesthetic, it depresses your nervous system and causes a temporary loss of bodily sensation – unlike most drugs ketamine makes you feel less rather than more.

As it's used for operating on animals and humans there's plenty of legally produced ketamine out there. The legally produced stuff comes in liquid form, which is injected; illegal ket appears as a grainy white powder which is snorted or bought as a tablet and swallowed.

Legal ketamine will be pure, but the illegally made stuff often has ephedrine added (commonly used for treatment of allergies and asthma). These are often passed off as ecstasy tablets.

The 2017/18 British Crime Survey showed that 141,000 more people aged 16 to 59 had taken the drug in that period than in the previous year, and that it was mostly popular among people under the age of 25. It, too can be a killer: an ONS report claims that in 2016 there were 12 deaths for which ket was mentioned on the death certificate, with seven cases where it was the only drug mentioned. While the dangers of this Class B drug are not as significant as those of other drugs, ketamine still comes with its dangers and should be avoided. It is, after all, a horse tranquiliser!

The highs
Ketamine takes you out of yourself, almost literally. You'll feel completely detached from your body, and experience a loss of feeling. It can feel like you're floating, with the sensation that your mind and body have been separated.

On top of this ket offers an hallucinogenic trip in which you see things, with objects becoming distorted. This can include 'seeing' colours and 'hearing' sounds.

Users trip for up to an hour and feel the after-effects for a long time.

The lows
There are all sorts of problems that can be caused by the fact that some users find themselves completely unable to move when they're on the drug, and as you

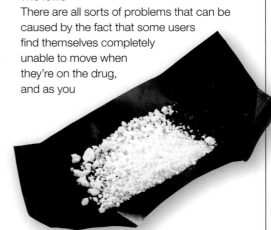

won't feel pain there's a high risk of causing yourself serious injury.

If taken in high enough doses this 'anaesthetic' effect can cause death – for example from inhaling vomit – or unconsciousness.

There are many other dangers with taking ketamine – it can cause depression and panic attacks, and can make existing mental health problems much, much worse. High doses, especially if taken with other depressant drugs such as alcohol, can make breathing hard, suppress your heart and in turn lead to unconsciousness.

Users may need to keep taking more and more to maintain the same level of buzz, further increasing the chances of serious problems each time it's taken.

MEPHEDRONE

Mephedrone (also known as 'Mcat, or 'meow meow') first burst on to the scene just over a decade ago as a legal alternative to amphetamines like ecstasy or speed, with dealers calling it 'plant food', 'bath salts' or 'research chemicals' in order to get round the law. 'Not for human consumption' they claimed. Cue hysteria in the media and some funny moments when newsreaders tried to say 'meow meow' with a straight face. Hilarity aside, mephedrone is a serious issue. In fact, the reason it hit the news in the first place was thanks to an increasing number of reported deaths associated with the product. The drug was duly made illegal in 2010 – it's now a Class B drug – but it remains popular, despite its lethal reputation; in 2016, there were 15 deaths where the drug was mentioned as a cause and two cases where it was the only drug taken, according to ONS figures.

The drug comes as a white, off-white or yellowish powder. Purity of the drug is a big issue and it's hard to tell what it is you're buying. Products might claim to be one thing but contain all sorts of other things – mephedrone is often mixed with other cathinones and caffeine.

People usually snort it, but sometimes also swallow it in wraps of paper ('bombs'). Occasionally it's taken as a pill.

It is still classified as a Class B drug under the Misuse of Drugs Act, but before this you could get hold of mephedrone on the Internet or in so-called 'head-shops'. Now dealers use some sneaky tactics to avoid getting caught, namely advertising the drug as 'plant food' and 'not for human consumption'.

The highs

With the drug being so new, reportage on the effects of mephedrone relies on stories from users. Most people say it's not unlike taking amphetamines, ecstasy or cocaine, giving the user a sense of euphoria and well-being. Users claim to become more alert, confident and talkative.

The lows

Like many drugs of this nature mephedrone has a serious effect on the heart, with users telling stories of heart palpitations (that's an irregular or racing heartbeat). It tends to get rid of your appetite, and nausea and vomiting are common, especially if mixed with cannabis or alcohol.

Obviously, snorting powder causes problems for your nose, throat and mouth, with burns or cuts caused by the chemicals, which can often lead to nosebleeds.

WHAT HAPPENS IF YOU GET CAUGHT WITH DRUGS?

Obviously, using and possessing most of the drugs mentioned is illegal, and so comes with legal consequences, so it's worth knowing what will happen to you if you get caught.

CLASS A

With these being considered the worst drugs, the penalties associated with them are obviously the harshest. For possession you can get seven years in prison and/or an unlimited fine, and for producing or supplying it you can get a life sentence and/or a fine. Is it really worth the risk of ruining your whole life?

CLASS B

These obviously have lower penalties than Class A drugs but they're still very serious. For possession you will get five years and/or a fine. Supplying can bag you up to 14 years in prison, an unlimited fine or both. If a Class B drug is prepared for injection it counts as a Class A substance.

CLASS C

These carry the lowest penalties with up to two years and/or a fine for possession. But for supplying you get the same punishment as for Class B drugs.

Less serious offences are usually handled in the magistrates' courts, where sentences aren't allowed to be over six months and/or a £5,000 fine, or three months and/or a fine. Despite maximum penalties being harsh only one in five of those convicted get a custodial sentence, and even fewer actually go to prison. Most get fines of £50 or less.

First aid

There are so many ways you can injure yourself, especially if there's booze involved. Accidents happen a lot from drunken falls and sports injuries to dodgy DIY and kitchen mishaps. Having a little bit of first aid knowledge can make all the difference. In many cases a little knowhow can stop a minor situation from becoming a massive one.

Here are a few simple tips and techniques that can go as far as saving lives:

Home first aid kit

As the Scout motto says, be prepared! You can injure yourself or get ill at any time, so it's worth being ready for it. You should keep simple first aid supplies in the house (or your room) to cover most minor accidents and ailments. These should include:

■ Painkillers (paracetamol, ibuprofen).
■ A selection of plasters, elastic bandages, cotton wool and assorted dressings.
■ Mild laxatives.
■ Indigestion remedy (for example antacids).
■ Travel sickness tablets.
■ Sunscreen (SPF30 or higher).
■ Thermometer.
■ Tweezers and sharp scissors.

THINGS TO REMEMBER

■ Store the first aid kit in a dry, secure place.
■ You might think it sounds like the best place to keep it, but don't keep it in the bathroom. The damp can damage the medicines and the bandages.
■ Always read the instructions and don't exceed the recommended dose of medicines.
■ Don't keep or use anything past its expiry date.

Things you shouldn't do (common mistakes)

What do you think you should do in an emergency? Everyone has their own ideas, mainly from the television! Here are a few common first aid mistakes people make:

■ **Don't be scared to dial 999** If you or a friend is injured and you're not sure what to do, it's probably a good idea to leave it to someone who does.
■ **Don't add yourself to the injury list** If you put yourself in danger, mess up and get injured, the emergency services will have two casualties to deal with instead of one. Before helping anybody check that the area is safe. If you're unsure, stay out of it until the professionals arrive.
■ **Don't feed the victim** There's a chance you could choke them! If, for example, they've had a stroke or a head injury there's a high likelihood of this happening.
■ **Don't leave drunks lying on their back** They're not in control of their body and could easily choke on their tongue or their own vomit. Stay with them and shout to get help.

First aid basics

If you can deal with minor injuries without calling an ambulance the emergency services would be very grateful – they have enough to worry about without helping out a student who's burnt himself on a cooker.

BURNS

1 Run the burn area under cold water to cool it down. Be patient, this can take up to ten minutes. If the burn is bigger than the injured person's own palm send someone to call an ambulance.

2 Take off watches, jewellery or anything else that can constrict the skin once it begins to swell from the burn. This includes shoes and necklaces.

3 If clothes are sticking to the skin, don't remove them.

4 Cover the burn with a non-fluffy material – you want to protect it and not get fluff in the wound. Cling film is ideal.

5 Don't burst any blisters or apply creams.

6 If the burn is severe there's likely to be a loss of blood pressure. Lay the victim down and raise their legs. This will help keep blood available to all the vital organs, like the heart, kidneys, lungs and brain.

HEAVY BLEEDING

If you have a cut or wound that needs a little more than a plaster, here's what to do:

1 Lay the person down. Usually bleeding from a vein is slow and all you should need to do is press the wound with a clean cloth and raise the bleeding limb above the level of the heart. This should stop the bleeding. Get them to a hospital.

2 Arterial bleeds (from an artery) are a different matter. You'll definitely notice one of these – the blood is bright red and spurts out everywhere, each heartbeat producing a little blood geyser.

3 Press a cloth to the wound and make sure it's held down firmly. If you have to leave the victim make sure the cloth is secure with a shirt or a towel.

4 Raise the person's legs and arms to keep the blood pressure up. There'll be some seepage, but you could save their life. Get them to a hospital ASAP.

EYE INJURIES

Eyes are pretty useful, and while they're seriously tough things can still go wrong and damage them. Things can get poked in there and all sorts of stuff can get stuck. Here's what to do to save an eye:

1 Lay the person down on their back and examine the eye. Only wash the eye if there's nothing obviously stuck to it that shouldn't be and there's no open wound.

2 Place a loose pad over the eye, held in place with a bandage.

3 Take them to the hospital.

BROKEN BONES

1 Keep the injured person still. Keep the limb steady and supported with your hands.

2 Cover any wounds with a non-fluffy material or dressing. Press as hard as required (without damaging the break) to stop the bleeding. Bandage the dressing on to the limb. Send someone to call an ambulance immediately.

3 If a leg is broken, tie both legs together, with rolled up magazines or a piece of wood between them. Start by tying the ankles and knees together first and then move closer to the broken bone.

4 For an arm or collarbone break fasten the arm to the body.

5 Check that hands and feet are warm by squeezing a nail to see if the colour returns to them. If not, loosen the bandages a little.

6 Check the bandages every 15 minutes, as swelling can tighten them.

Chapter 5
Relationships

The most important thing at university is the people around you – they will make or break your time on campus.
It is important that you get the most out of your new friends without losing ties to the relationships at 'home' (old friends, old flames and family). This chapter will help you get the most out of your relationships while on campus ...

Long-distance romance

A big worry for many people starting university is keeping a relationship going once you're both in far-flung corners of the country.

Just follow these simple rules:

1 Be honest

It's a bit of a relationship cliché to say 'honesty is the best policy', but it's a massive necessity in a long-distance relationship.

If you've made friends with a guy or girl at uni and are spending a lot of time with them, be honest and don't hide the fact! If you're being open and not doing anything wrong the level of trust will rise.

2 Stay happy

This sounds silly, but being happy with your choice of university and the route you've taken is important. Don't sit in your room missing your other half, pining over them – get out there and live a little (you'll never get that first year of uni experience back).

3 Quality time

Make sure you don't waste the time that you do have together. Don't just sit in

watching telly, get out into the world and create some decent memories.

4 It's good to talk!

Try to talk to each other every day. If you don't actually speak you can at least message them on WhatsApp, or drop them an email. There's really no reason to ever be out of each other's lives.

5 Keep the flame burning

You don't need to make overblown romantic gestures every day, but simple things like a 'Morning!' text to show your partner you're thinking about them goes a long way.

6 Don't cheat, leave

It's a saying to live by! If the relationship is right you should really have no need to cheat – despite all the temptations that university will more than likely throw your way. You'll both be surrounded by new, exciting and most probably attractive people, and you're miles and miles apart, so starting at uni can be a sink or swim moment. You'll realise either that no one compares to your other half, or that there are people you like more – which is fine too. Just be honest about it. Discuss it and make the best decision for you. Just do your partner the courtesy of talking to them before you play away.

Following these rules and putting time and effort in, if it's 'meant to be', should be enough to keep the relationship afloat.

New relationships and friends

Freshers' Week is a strange time. Everyone is in the same boat. Everything's new, you're all surrounded by new people, and most people will be going out of their way to be your mate. Take the friendships you make during this time with a pinch of salt.

As the weeks progress, people settle in and the drink-induced friendliness subsides, you may drift apart as you find out that you don't really have that much in common. As time goes on people naturally form stronger friendships with people who have similar tastes, outlooks on life and interests as themselves. The key is not to take the collapse of early friendships personally – they're a very common occurrence. It's a well-known fact that by the end of university most people barely talk to the people they were friends with in the first term!

A lot of people see starting university as a time to reinvent themselves. No one knows you, or what you've done in the past. Of course, these days it's much harder to act a particular way when your whole life is on social media for all to see! The key to having good friendships at university is to be yourself. Don't change who you are to fit in, and don't try to make people like you by being something you're not. If you like fantasy role-play games or collecting stamps don't be ashamed of it, embrace it – you'll be surprised just how many people have the same interests as you.

FAMILY RELATIONSHIPS

Starting at university you'll probably be jumping for joy at the freedom from your parents. You can do what you like when you like, and they won't even know about it, never mind give you a telling off for leaving dirty dishes in your room.

But this freedom doesn't mean you should neglect your family while away on campus. Family relationships are the most important in your life – no matter what happens they'll more than likely be there to support you.

I'm not saying that you need to call or text your mum every day, but a little contact – if only to show that you're still alive – won't go amiss and will mean the world to her. You might feel like an adult but to mummy-dearest you're still her baby, and without any news she'll be imagining the worst about your new drug habit, drink-fuelled orgies and squalid living quarters. For most of you none of that will be the case (the rest of you know who you are) and it's a good idea to let the parents know.

Little things like remembering birthdays and visiting home for family events are important, especially when it comes to grandparents – you don't want to miss a big birthday only to lose them soon after. Living with family regrets isn't a nice experience. So just because you've started a new chapter of your life doesn't mean you should neglect the people who've been important in your life up till now, and this is more than likely going to be your family.

It might not seem like it but almost everyone is as nervous as you are, so the last thing you want to do is be shy. It might be hard, but you should introduce yourself to people – remember, they know nothing about you and you have nothing to worry about. Sitting in your room waiting for people to come to you will see you sitting on your lonesome for quite some time. Make the first move and say hello at every opportunity – people you want to be friends with and that attractive person of the opposite sex you can't stop staring at.

If you have interests (everyone does) seek out the societies and clubs that will be full of people who like what you like.

As a fresher make sure you get down to the freshers' fair and check out what's on offer. Don't limit your friendship circle to the people in your flat – there's a chance you might end up hating each other after three months.

Make sure people have your mobile number and add you on social media etc. It's easier now more than ever to keep in touch, arrange parties and drinking sessions and keep in the loop, so you have no excuse for being a social loner at uni.

How to make new friends

■ **Be sociable** Get out there! Convince yourself to say yes to as much as possible. Not everything, but the good and non-life-threatening suggestions.

■ **Leave your uni door open** Who knows who you might attract in with the music you're playing etc? But don't take

this too literally, there are some moments when your door should be shut ...

■ **Join clubs and societies** Are most people bored of you spending endless hours talking about your love of fossils, *Star Trek*, marbles, baking, whatever? Join a load of people who also want to spend hours talking about it.

■ **Organise stuff** Plan things with your new flatmates, course mates and society mates. Have flat meals, go for course drinks after lectures, organise a film night, go clubbing – make sure you do plenty of stuff to bond with your new buddies.

■ **Be open-minded and try new things** Uni is the perfect place to try new things and get to know new types of people. There's a good chance you'll be a completely different person at the end than you were at the beginning, and this will be largely down to the new and interesting people you'll meet. This isn't school, there aren't 'cool' kids and 'geeks' (or whatever pointless social groups teenagers use to segregate themselves). Things are much more fluid. Embrace this and who knows who you might meet?

Now there's every chance that some of these new friendships will develop into something more. You might find yourself wanting to have a, let's say more 'special' kind of friendship with someone. This is going to be a lot different than before – at uni you're completely free of your parents and able to do what you want. Unfortunately, doing what you want can sometimes lead to you getting in a bit deep or looking like some kind of serious stalker. So:

■ **Take your time** By this I mean in getting to know people. At the start of uni everything and everyone seems new and exciting, so get to know people properly before jumping to the next level of relationship.

■ **Don't settle** Don't settle for the first person that shows interest in you. Get to know people and keep your options open. This doesn't mean putting it about! Getting into a relationship is a big step and can be a whole lot of drama to get out of. So be sure.

- **Don't become a relationship recluse** Yes, your new other half is 'amazing' and you want to spend all your time with them, but don't forget about all the other things that make uni life amazing. Don't neglect your friends, social life and course in favour of your relationship – you'll regret it and in the long run it'll be something that becomes a problem. Having things outside of your relationship is a healthy necessity in making it work.

- **Don't confuse sex with love** Just because you've slept with someone doesn't mean it will go further. If the other person is interested in getting more from you they'll get in touch. Don't turn into some sort of stalker, bothering them every day. Sex doesn't mean there are deeper feelings involved. Also, in getting into a relationship don't confuse physical attraction with something deeper. For a relationship to last there needs to be something more once the initial physical excitement dies down.

- **Talk it through** Are you starting to develop feelings for someone? Do you think they may feel the same? Talk to them about it.

Maybe don't profess your undying love for them, but ask them out for a drink and tell them how you feel. This way it's out in the open – worst-case scenario is that they don't have any interest in you, but your friendship can stay intact. The best-case scenario is that they feel the same and you can look to take things further. Don't just keep it to yourself as you watch the object of your desire get it on with other people just because you've been too scared to mention it.

- **Be honest** Be honest about your feelings, to yourself and the other person. If you're not interested or are having doubts discuss it openly and put all your cards on the table.

Let's talk about sex ...

If you're going to be having sex at university, and let's face it most people will be, it's worth knowing your stuff so you can have all the fun without the nasty repercussions. The last thing you want to be taking home at Christmas is an STI or an unwanted pregnancy!

Safety first (contraception)

By the time you start university you should know all about contraception. It's not like the information isn't out there! But, shockingly, there are a lot of people who are clueless about safe sex. Let's put that right.

Many misunderstandings and myths exist about contraception, and that puts people at risk. Take condoms, for instance. When 2,200 students were asked about condoms by the Terrence Higgins Trust in 2007 the answers were alarming. As well as many people not knowing how to put one on, 16 per cent thought that using two condoms was safer and seven people thought they could be washed and used again. Yet others believed that other forms of contraception, such as the pill, could protect against sexually transmitted diseases (STIs).

Let's get this straight, then. When you use a (male) latex condom properly it is 98 per cent effective against STIs and pregnancy. That's pretty safe... Condoms with spermicide are most effective and many are also lubricated to make sex more comfortable. Spermicide-/lubricant-free condoms are also available, as well as a whole pile of other varieties (coloured, textured and flavoured).

Condoms that are made from polyurethane (not latex) are just as safe and are an effective alternative if you suffer from a latex allergy.

Female condoms are also made from polyurethane. The female version is a larger version of the male one and is fitted inside the vagina before sex. This is still pretty safe, being 95 per cent effective if used without a hitch.

Of course there are other forms of contraception – the oral or implanted hormone pill, the coil – but these do not protect against STIs, so for complete peace of mind it's best to stick with johnnies, especially if you have multiple partners.

Getting condoms

Getting hold of condoms is very, very easy. They're more than likely going to be available free from your university health centre, so definitely look into that. If not, there'll be plenty of other local family planning centres and young people centres that might be able to give you some.

They can also be bought in supermarkets, chemists, pubs, bars, petrol stations and public toilets, so there's no need not to have one. Make sure that all condoms have a BSI kitemark or a CE mark on the packet – this means they've been tested to a high safety standard.

IN CASE OF EMERGENCY

Emergency contraception (aka 'the morning after pill') is a safe and effective way of preventing pregnancy when no contraception was used or regular contraception has failed. You need to take tablets within 72 hours of having sex. They are available free from GPs, family planning clinics, NHS walk-in centres and pharmacies.

Condoms aren't perfect

Obviously, condoms aren't perfect. On rare occasions they can slip off or split, especially if you're a bit rough putting one on or if you have sharp fingernails and pointy jewellery.

They're also weakened by oil-based lubricants, so can be destroyed if they come in contact with stuff like body lotion, baby oil, suntan lotion or Vaseline.

One of the major downfalls (and the one that usually results in a condom not being used) is that you'll have to interrupt the sexual moment to put a condom on. But all in all it's a small price to pay for protection against STIs and not getting pregnant.

Contraceptive methods with possibility of user failure

The methods in this table must be used correctly to achieve the effectiveness stated.

	Combined pill	Progestogen-only pill	Male condom	Female condom	Diaphragm or cap	Natural family planning (NFP)
HOW IT WORKS	Contains two hormones, oestrogen and progestogen, which stop ovulation.	Contains the hormone progestogen, which thickens the cervical mucus, and stops sperm getting near the egg.	Barrier method. The condom covers the penis and stops sperm entering the vagina.	Barrier method. The condom lines the vagina and stops sperm entering.	Barrier method. A rubber or silicone cap covers the cervix to keep sperm out of the womb. Used with spermicidal cream or jelly.	Fertile and infertile times in the menstrual cycle are identified.
PROS	Can reduce PMS, period pain and bleeding. Protects against cancer of the womb and ovary.	Can be used when breast-feeding. More suitable for older smokers than the combined pill.	Wide choice and easy availability. Provides some protection against sexually transmitted infections. Under male control.	Can be put in before sex. Provides some protection against sexually transmitted infections.	Can be put in before sex. Provides some protection against sexually transmitted infections.	Freedom from side-effects. Awareness of fertile times can be used for planning pregnancies as well as avoiding them.
CONS	Increased risk of breast and cervical cancer. Increased risk of thrombosis (blood clots).	May produce irregular periods with bleeding in between. May be less effective in women weighing over 70 kg (11 stone).	Need to stop to put it on. Can split or come off if not used correctly. Need to withdraw while still erect.	If not inserted in advance, need to stop to put it in. Need to make sure that the penis enters correctly.	If not inserted in advance, need to stop to put it in. Can provoke cystitis in some users.	Method must be taught by a qualified teacher. Users must abstain from sex, or use a barrier method, during the fertile period.
REMARKS	Smokers over 35 should not use it (risk of thrombosis).	Must be taken at exactly the same time each day (to within 3 hours).	Do not re-use. Must be put on before genital contact occurs. Do not use oil-based lubricants on latex condoms.	Do not re-use. Must be put in before genital contact occurs. Expensive to buy, but can be obtained free at some family planning clinics.	Must be correctly fitted, and fit must be checked every 12 months. Must be put in before genital contact occurs.	There are various different methods of indicating fertility. Effectiveness is highest when using several indicators.
EFFECTIVENESS	over 99%	99%	98%	95%	92% to 96%	up to 98%

* Effectiveness is expressed as the percentage of women who will not get pregnant with each year of correct use of a particular contraceptive method. So if the effectiveness is 99%, 1 woman in 100 will get pregnant in a year. Using no contraception at all, 80 to 90 women out of 100 will get pregnant in a year.

Contraceptive methods with no possibility of user failure

The effectiveness of the methods in this table does not depend on the user.

	Contraceptive injection	Implant	Intrauterine system (IUS)	Intrauterine device (IUD)	Female sterilisation	Male sterilisation (vasectomy)
HOW IT WORKS	The hormone progestogen is slowly released, stopping ovulation and thickening the cervical mucus.	An implant is placed under the skin. It releases the hormone progestogen, stopping ovulation and thickening the cervical mucus.	A small plastic device is inserted into the womb. It releases the hormone progestogen, thickening the cervical mucus.	A small plastic and copper device is inserted into the womb. It stops sperm meeting an egg, or fertilised eggs implanting.	The fallopian tubes are cut, sealed or otherwise blocked. The egg cannot meet the sperm.	The tubes carrying the sperm from each testis are cut or blocked. There are no sperm in the semen.
PROS	Single injection lasts for 8 or 12 weeks. Protects against cancer of the womb and ovary.	Single implant works for 3 years. Quickly reversed at any time.	Single insertion lasts for 5 years. Quickly reversed at any time. Periods are normally lighter and less painful.	Single insertion lasts for up to 10 years (depending on model). Effective immediately.	Permanent. No known long-term side-effects.	Permanent. No known long-term side-effects. Minor operation under local anaesthetic.
CONS	Fertility may take a year to return after stopping the injections. Periods may become irregular or stop. Other side-effects, including weight gain, in some users.	Periods may become irregular or stop. Other side-effects, including weight gain, in some users.	Irregular light bleeding for the first 3 months is common; sometimes this lasts longer. Other side-effects in some users.	Periods may become heavier, longer and more painful. Not suitable for women at risk of catching a sexually transmitted infection.	Invasive surgical procedure under general anaesthetic. Small possibility (1 in 200) of tubes rejoining and restoring fertility.	Expect some swelling and discomfort after the operation. Very small possibility (1 in 2,000) of tubes rejoining.
REMARKS	Effects cannot be stopped until the injection runs out.	Usually inserted and removed using a local anaesthetic.	Useful for women with very heavy or painful periods.	IUD insertion can also be used as emergency contraception.	Should be assumed to be irreversible. Other contraception must be used until the first period after sterilisation.	Should be assumed to be irreversible. Other contraception must be used until there have been two consecutive negative sperm tests.
EFFECTIVENESS	over 99%	over 99%	over 99%	98% or better	99.5%	99.95%

* Effectiveness is expressed as the percentage of women who will not get pregnant with each year of correct use of a particular contraceptive method. So if the effectiveness is 99%, 1 woman in 100 will get pregnant in a year. Using no contraception at all, 80 to 90 women out of 100 will get pregnant in a year.

Have I got an STI?

So you've ignored the safe sex advice, or something has gone wrong and there's something funny going on downstairs. There's a good chance it could be one of those pesky sexually transmitted diseases (STIs). What should you do to deal with it?

DON'T IGNORE IT

Pretending there's nothing going on won't make it go away! Something is happening and you need to admit there's a problem and deal with it quickly. When it comes to health, denial is a risk that's just not worth taking. Also, it might be nothing to worry about and it's worth looking into it to put your mind at ease.

ASK FOR HELP

Go to your GP or find out where your nearest GUM (genitourinary medicine) clinic is, and when they open, then get yourself down there ASAP. Don't put it off!

It might be embarrassing, frightening even, but these people have seen it all before, probably many times every day, and they're there to help. You don't even need to give your real name – it's confidential! It's all free, so get the right diagnosis, good advice and the treatment you need – it's a pretty good deal. They can also give you free condoms and advice about safer sex, so you can make sure you don't need to visit them again.

OWN UP

This is much more scary than visiting a clinic. It will be hard, but your partner (or partners) needs to know! Tell anyone you might have passed the infection on to – letting them know is the right thing to do.

Don't get angry and blame the person who gave you the infection; safe sex is the responsibility of both the people involved. It doesn't mean they cheated on you, as it's possible that one of you could have been carrying the infection for a long time without knowing about it.

Don't lie to the doctor – telling them you have a chest infection when you know you have an STI isn't going to help you at all.

DO AS YOU'RE TOLD

Do what the doctors tell you! If they give you antibiotics, finish the course of tablets. If you don't the infection could come back. Don't have sex until you're given the all-clear.

DEAL WITH IT

You could be unlucky and catch one of the infections that can't be cleared up with antibiotics, and you'll need support and advice to deal with it. GUM clinics have counselling available and there are specialist charities and agencies that can help too.

THINGS YOU MIGHT GET: COMMON STIs

Chlamydia

If you're going to get anything, it's most likely to be this. Chlamydia is one of the most common STIs in the UK, and most people who have it don't notice any symptoms, and won't have a clue they're infected. Chlamydia is sneaky like that.

The good news is that diagnosing it is simply done with a urine test or a swab of the affected area. It's also easily treated with antibiotics. It's well worth getting it seen to quickly as well, because unchecked it can cause some serious long-term health problems.

Symptoms

In most cases people won't notice the symptoms (50% of men and 70–80% of women don't have any), but chlamydia does have some signs to look out for:

Women

Girls with chlamydia may notice the following symptoms:

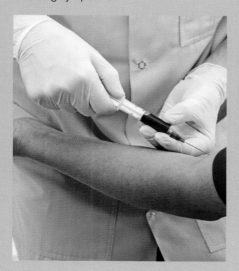

- Cystitis (pain when passing urine).
- A change in vaginal discharge.
- Lower abdominal pain.
- Pain and/or bleeding during sexual intercourse.
- Bleeding after sex.
- Bleeding between periods, or heavier periods.

Men

Guys with chlamydia may notice the following symptoms:

- A white, cloudy or watery discharge from the tip of the penis.
- Pain when passing urine.
- Pain in the testicles.

What it can do to you

If left untreated in women the infection can spread to the womb and cause pelvic inflammatory disease (PID), which is a major cause of infertility, ectopic pregnancy and miscarriage.

It's no less serious in men. Untreated they're at risk of complications such as inflamed and swollen testicles, reactive arthritis and infertility.

THE NATIONAL CHLAMYDIA SCREENING PROGRAMME

Luckily, if you're under 25 you can get a free, confidential test with the National Chlamydia Screening Programme (NCSP). This is available in loads of places including some pharmacies, and has even been available in some bars and nightclubs.

In some areas testing kits can also be provided through the post, which you can order online.

Genital warts

These are as unpleasant as they sound. Genital warts are tiny fleshy bumps, growths and changes to the skin that appear round your genitals or anus. Really not nice! It comes from a viral skin infection by the name of human papillomavirus (HPV). You don't even need to have sex to catch this little beauty; no, this is spread by skin-to-skin contact.

People get these a lot! After chlamydia they come in at number two on the chart of most common STIs in the UK. The student age group also get them the most, it being common for men aged between 20 and 24 and females aged between 16 and 19.

But not to worry, there are treatments to combat them, such as creams and freezing them off (called cryotherapy). However, many treatments can take up to three months before they're fully effective.

SYMPTOMS

Unlike many other STIs you'll notice genital warts, and the symptoms are pretty obvious.

Women

They usually start as small, gritty-feeling lumps that then grow in size. You're most likely to find them around your vulva (the opening to the vagina), anus and vagina. In fewer cases they're found on the cervix (the neck of the womb) and at the opening of the urethra.

Men

In guys they often look like the warts some people get on their hands – firm and sticking out, with a rough surface. You'll notice if you get these on your genitals! You're most likely to notice them on your penis (usually just below the foreskin) or around your anus. They can also be found on the glans (head of the penis), inside the urethra, under the foreskin and on the scrotum. They can come as one wart or in a cluster that looks a bit like a cauliflower.

WHAT IT CAN DO TO YOU

Most of the time genital warts are painless, but some people experience itchiness or irritation, especially with ones around the anus.

In really extreme cases a few people have experienced bleeding from the warts during sex. It's generally not advised to have sex until the warts are fully healed.

Warts near or inside the urethra (the tube connected to the bladder) can make it hard to pee.

Gonorrhoea

Traditionally known as 'the clap', this nasty little STI is easily passed around and is caused by a bacteria called neisseria gonorrhoeae or gonococcus. These bacteria live in the discharge from the penis and vaginal fluid in infected men and women, so any form of sex passes it on very easily. This is so contagious that it can even be passed on from a pregnant woman to her baby.

If you don't use barrier contraception there's a high risk of catching this. Again, students are right in the firing line for it, with the most affected age group being 16–24-year-olds (in 2008 they accounted for 47% of all new gonorrhoea cases).

Luckily it's easily identified with a simple swab test and can be treated with antibiotics. If left untreated it can have some serious effects on your health, and just because you've been treated successfully for it once doesn't mean you can't catch it again.

SYMPTOMS

Most people don't notice any symptoms so it can go untreated and unnoticed for quite a long time. But there are some symptoms to look out for:

Women
- An unusual discharge from the vagina, which may be thick, and green or yellow in colour.

- Pain when passing urine.
- Pain or tenderness in the lower abdominal area (this is less common).
- Bleeding between periods or heavier periods (this is less common).

Men
- An unusual discharge from the tip of the penis, which may be white, yellow or green.
- Pain or a burning sensation when urinating.
- Inflammation (swelling) of the foreskin.
- Pain or tenderness in the testicles or prostate gland (this is rare).

Men and women
- Infection in the rectum, which may cause pain, discomfort or discharge.
- Infection in the throat, which does not usually have any symptoms.
- Infection in the eyes, which can cause pain, swelling, irritation and discharge (conjunctivitis).

WHAT IT CAN DO TO YOU

If not treated, early gonorrhoea can lead to serious health problems and complications. The more times you get it the more chance you have of it becoming serious.

In women it can spread to your reproductive organs and cause something called pelvic inflammatory disease (PIS), which can lead to long-term pelvic pain and infertility (that's no kids, ever). In guys it can cause a painful infection in the testicles and the prostate gland, which can lead to infertility. It can also cause a whole host of things, including:

- Inflammation (swelling) of the joints and tendons.

- Skin lesions (rash).
- Inflammation around the brain and spinal cord (meningitis) and the heart, which can be fatal.

Genital herpes

This is definitely one of the least pleasant STIs (not that any are what you'd call nice). Genital herpes gives you painful blisters on your genitals and the areas around them. It's caused by the herpes simplex virus (HSV) type 1 or type 2, and can be passed on to others through intimate sexual contact. HSV can affect any mucous membrane (moist lining), especially those found in the mouth, anus and vagina – which means sex is one of its most common causes of spreading.

When around the mouth, HSV can cause blister-like lesions called cold sores. If you suffer from these, avoid kissing and oral sex, as this can also spread the disease.

It's a long-term condition, with most people having it reappear several times – on average at a rate of four to five times in the first two years after infection. But over time the frequency of attacks decreases and the condition becomes less severe with each subsequent occurrence.

This is becoming a bit of a theme, but once again this STI is most common amongst the student age group, that's 20–24-year-olds. The bad news is that there's no cure for genital herpes, but symptoms can be controlled.

SYMPTOMS

Symptoms may not appear until months (or years) after you become infected. If you do experience symptoms when you first get it you'll notice them four to seven days after you've been exposed to the virus.

Women
On first infection:
- Blisters and ulcers on the cervix (lower part of the womb).
- Vaginal discharge.
When it comes back:
- Blisters and ulcers on the cervix.

Men and women
On first infection:
- Painful red blisters that burst to leave open sores around your genitals, rectum (back passage), thighs and buttocks.
- Pain when you pass urine.
- A high temperature (fever) of 38°C (100.4°F) or above.
- A general feeling of being unwell, with aches and pains.
When it comes back:
- A tingling, burning or itching sensation around your genitals, and sometimes down your leg, before the blisters appear (this can signal the onset of a recurrent infection).
- Painful red blisters that soon burst to leave sores around your genitals, rectum (back passage), thighs and buttocks.

WHAT IT CAN DO TO YOU

In some rare cases the herpes blisters can become infected by other bacteria, and this can cause the condition to spread to other parts of the body.

In women herpes has been known to cause complications during pregnancy. It's also a condition that can be passed on to your baby – not the nicest first gift for your child, I think you'll agree.

Am I pregnant?

Let's move on to the other side effect of having sex – babies. Yes, if you're having sex there's a chance you could get pregnant.

For most women the first indication that they might be pregnant is missing their period, but to be entirely sure you'll need to take a pregnancy test. Other signs of pregnancy include:

- Sore breasts.
- Feeling sick or vomiting at any time of the day or night.
- Feeling very tired.
- Needing to wee often.

There are several options available to find out whether you're pregnant or not:

Your doctor

An appointment with your GP will help you to find out very quickly. They'll ask you to take a urine test, which will give you instant results. Your doctor can then offer you the support you need depending on the results and what decisions you make.

A pregnancy testing kit

Your local chemist will have a range of simple-to-use products which can identify the presence of a hormone in your urine that will show if you're pregnant or not. Consider who you can talk to after you check the results. It's important to have someone to rely on for support.

Chemist or health centre

You can take a urine sample to many Brook Advisory Centres (if you're under 25), contraceptive clinics, young people's clinics and many chemists for a free and confidential urine test. It's quick, with less chance of misinterpreting the results.

Do your research. Some organisations offer free pregnancy tests but don't believe in abortion, and may not give you all the information you need to help make the decision that's right for you.

MAKING THE RIGHT DECISION FOR YOU

The decision to have an abortion can be a very difficult one. There can be a lot of things to consider, so it's important that you get all of the necessary advice and information. Your GP is one of the best people to talk to about everything. You can also contact the Family Planning Association on their confidential number (0845 122 8690) or The Brook Advisory Centre on 0800 0185 023.

Understanding consent

With the rise of the Me Too movement and some high-profile cases coming to light, the sheer magnitude of the problem of rape and sexual assault faced by women (yes, it happens to men too, but statistically not to the same level) has been placed in the global spotlight.

Sadly, university campuses are very much not exempt from the issue, and there are countless incidences of assault. Over in the USA, the hard-hitting 2015 documentary *The Hunting Ground* made the discussion about campus assault more visible, while the case of Brock Turner shocked many with his, and his father's, defence of his attack on an unconscious girl, also in 2015. Here in the UK, as recently as November 2019 several female students claimed that Birmingham University had failed to investigate rape claims on campus.

So, as a quick Google will show you, assaults at university are not uncommon.

THE VICTIM IS NEVER TO BLAME

Let's make this crystal clear: no one is to blame for an assault apart from the person doing the assaulting. Nothing that anyone wears, says, does or thinks is responsible for an assault, unless they are the perpetrator. That should make things a lot easier to understand. Consent is not always clear-cut but who is to blame most certainly is.

All is not lost, though; it's a positive thing the conversation has changed. Groups such as Stop Rape on Campus, the

CONSENT UNDER THE INFLUENCE

The issue of consent becomes incredibly complicated when drink or drugs are involved. Drunk or high people are less able to negotiate sexual activity, and to give consent. On the flip side, people can be less able to get or respect consent. To clarify, if a person is drunk or high, they can't legally consent to sex and it is the responsibility of the other person to check they are OK before proceeding. If at any time you are unsure about this, stop. Having sex with someone who is so out of it they can't understand what is happening is rape or sexual assault. If you sexually assault someone, being drunk is not an excuse. You still committed a crime and there is no excuse.

visibility of Me Too and campaigning from the NUS have made it much easier for survivors to be heard. They have also raised the issue of 'consent', resulting in a much more active discussion about the issue, among both men and women. So, how can we all make sure everything is consensual?

What is consent?

Consent is agreeing to do something, so when it comes to sex it means agreeing to sexual activity – anything from kissing to penetrative sex. Getting and giving consent before (and during) sex will mean that everyone can enjoy it. Anything other than this is rape or sexual assault.

Consent is a two-way street of communication, which means that expressing 'enthusiastic consent' (indicating with words and body language that you are into it) can be as important as

actively seeking consent. This doesn't need to be mood-killing, over-blown conversations – some positive gestures and words should be enough.

The same goes for denying consent. The words you're likely to hear are self-explanatory ('no', 'stop', 'I'm not sure') but the body language can sometimes be more difficult to read. One thing people often get wrong is that they believe you have to say 'no' to not consent to sex. In fact, it can be done through body language, hand gestures or facial expressions. According to the Family Planning Association, you should look out for any of the following to indicate that consent is not being given:

- avoiding eye contact
- not suggesting any sexual activity
- pushing someone away
- avoiding touch
- shaking head no
- uncomfortable being naked
- crying and/or looking sad or fearful
- tense, stiff or closed arms and legs
- turning away from someone
- silence
- whimpering or a trembling voice

If you are unsure whether or not your partner is consenting, always ask them. And if you feel uncomfortable at any time know that you can remove consent. Remember, it is OK to change your mind. What's more, just because you consented before doesn't mean you need to consent again, and just because you agree to one activity doesn't mean everything is OK. In every situation, it is your body and you have the right to decide what happens. In every case, no means no.

Chapter 6
Leisure

Let's be honest, most people won't spend
all their time at university studying. The
good news is that on campus there is so
much going on you will never need to get
bored. University also gives you more
flexible time than you will ever have
again to explore the world. Here are a
few pointers on how to fill all
that opportunity.

Clubs and societies

At school and college you'll have gravitated towards people with the same interests as you (if you could find any, that is – it's not always easy to find people with the same love of Bavarian folk music). At university it's dead easy to find people into the same things as you through clubs and societies.

Basically students run their own clubs for other students who like what they like. And the array of clubs available is staggering – it's very unlikely that you won't find something to interest you. In general these clubs tend to centre around a particular activity or belief (usually religious or political).

To join, the only rule tends to be that you're a student at the university, although in some cases you're also expected to share the beliefs of the society you wish to participate in. If you want to join the Christian Union they'd prefer it if you believed in Christ, for instance – which makes sense really.

In general they're part of (and are overseen by) the students' union. Of course, you can always just start your own, but without any official backing it's not really a club/society, it's just a group of mates sitting around to discuss their favourite Avenger.

New fill societies will require the approval of the students' union, who'll make sure they maintain the beliefs and moral codes set down in the constitution.

Common student club and society types

- **Music** Maybe you're a 1975 fan looking to fawn over Matty Healy, or you just want to sit around and discuss the nuances of metalcore. Either way, there will be something for you. Universities also have many choirs, orchestras and bands to get involved with.
- **Political** Maybe you hate capitalism, maybe you love it. Maybe you're a raving Labour supporter or a rampant Tory Boy. Most types of political affiliation are catered for on campus, from the big mainstream parties down to fringe political ideas.

- **Religious** No matter what you believe in chances are you'll be able to find a society (or club) where you can sit around and believe in it in the company of other people.
- **Television and film** There's a wide variety of groups to watch, discuss and fawn over your favourites from the large and small screens. The same applies for books, theatre, arts – in fact anything to do with culture, really.
- **Debating** This can be similar to the political, but debating societies have arguments about all sorts of things. The most famous debating society is the Oxford Union and they've had everyone from Michael Jackson and the Dalai Lama to Katie Price and BNP leader Nick Griffin through their doors to have a good old debate about various issues.

BIZARRE SOCIETIES

There really is a society for (almost) everything. This is wonderful. If you think your weird and wonderful interests won't make you friends, you are probably wrong!

Here are just five of the most bizarre student societies in the UK:

1. BRUM DINE WITH ME (University of Birmingham)
Not that weird exactly, but a winner on the pun alone, this is based on the popular Channel 4 cooking competition series *Come Dine With Me*. Over six weeks, four or five student strangers cook for each other and judge the results.

2. GUS APPRECIATION (University of Greenwich, London)
This union has a cat. That cat is called Gus – he is awesome. So awesome in fact that this group get together simply to appreciate him.

3. 20 MINUTE (Manchester University)
Injecting some spontaneity into life, this society doesn't let its members know where its socials are until 20 minutes before it starts! Then it's a mad dash to wherever that is. Exciting!

4. ASSASSINS (Durham University)
Sounds violent, doesn't it? But not to worry – there aren't students running around campus knocking people off. No, this is all about mock assassinations. Players are assigned targets whom they have to hunt down and assassinate with fake weapons such as cardboard knives and water pistols – while also being hunted. The winner is the last assassin left standing.

5. SHEILA AND HER DOG (University of Cambridge)
This one really is bizarre. It's all about regressing back to childhood (every member is considered six years old at meetings) and each meeting starts by ceremonially dropping a penguin called Alan. They drink hot chocolate, read children's stories, eat sweets and play with teddy bears. Oh and they all wear dressing gowns!

Fabulous Footlights

One of the most well-known university clubs and societies is Cambridge University's Footlights Dramatic Club, referred to by those in the know simply as Footlights. It's a student society that's churned out the ridiculously talented at an impressive rate since it started in 1893. You may have heard of a few of them. Most recently Simon Bird (yes, Will from *The Inbetweeners*) moved through the Footlights' ranks, and he sits atop an impressive table of alumni.

Three of the Monty Python team were in Footlights (John Cleese, Eric Idle and Graham Chapman), and other former members include actress Emma Thompson, Ali G and Borat creator Sacha Baron Cohen, Stephen Fry, comedy duo Mitchell and Webb, and *IT Crowd* actor and *Submarine* director Richard Ayoade.

If you're lucky enough to be a member of this student club you're more than likely surrounded by some of our future stars!

A student society that's churned out the ridiculously talented at an impressive rate since it started in 1893.

Student media

Student media is something very close to my heart. Without it I wouldn't be sitting here writing this book, and I wouldn't have done half the things that I have done over the past ten years.

So what is student media? Well, it's pretty self-explanatory – it's media made by students. All campuses have some form of media, including newspapers, magazines, radio stations and even, in some cases, their own television channels.

If you ever fancied yourself as a journalist, radio presenter or TV cameraman, university is the perfect place to step up to the plate and give it a go. Although being part of student media can be time-consuming and a lot of hard work, the rewards – and fun – can massively outweigh that extra workload.

You may wonder why on earth you should get involved in student media. Well, to cut a long story short, it will help get you a job. Working in student media will give you many transferable skills that are attractive to employers no matter what industry you want to work in. These include teaching you the value of hard work, commitment, meeting deadlines and how to operate in teams under pressure. Learning what it means to be drained and mentally exhausted after a few days of poring over words or a video edit will give you an advantage, and you'll come to understand that the end product is worth the stress and seeing your creation being consumed is the best feeling. Working in student media can uncover interests and skills you

didn't even know you had, like me setting up *The National Student*. Without our involvement in our student magazines we'd have taken very different paths.

Many top radio DJs learned their trade on their uni station. For example, Radio 1 DJ Greg James started off doing several shows at University of East Anglia station Livewire, where he became the station manager in 2006. The media is literally full of people who started their careers on campus.

It's a well-known fact that student media is the perfect place to start your media career, giving you the right start and a safe environment in which to try out new things and develop your skills.

But it's not all about employability. This sounds tragically clichéd but you will make great friends in such a hectic and passionate environment – people who will be friends for life. I still speak to the co-hosts of my radio shows and people I worked with on *The National Student* and they are some of my favourite people ever!

Most student media in the UK is organised, controlled and funded by each university's students' union, who pay for the running costs and provide the facilities. Although on many campuses there are harmonious relationships between union sabbaticals and campus media, the wishes of the union can cause tension and frustrations.

Sabbaticals may see their media simply as a tool to promote themselves rather than the best interests of the students on campus.

But with the unions paying for much of the production costs of all media and with an elected sabbatical being constitutionally responsible for the media's output, shouldn't they be allowed to ensure that everything reflects the uni correctly and in a positive light? Is the representation of the union more important than giving students what they need in terms of information?

It's a debate that's never likely to be settled, but it's something you should be aware of if you decide to get involved. Working in student media, you'll not please everyone all of the time, and you may have to fight to create the media you want – but

It's a well-known fact that student media is the perfect place to start your media career

for many people this is part of the excitement, and it certainly prepares you for all sorts of conflicts when you step out into the real world.

MAKE FRIENDS IN HIGH PLACES

I started off writing for student media at the University of Lincoln, where I also worked on the radio station Siren FM, before launching the UK's first independent national student publication – *The National Student* – back in 2003. This helped people start their career in media, until it was shut down by its owners in 2019. During its time in publication, we helped to spark the careers of people at the *Daily Mail*, *NME*, *Heat*, the *BBC*, the *Guardian*, *Metal Hammer*, *Pitchfork* and the *Times* as well as authors, filmmakers and photographers.

In some cases there are thriving student magazines, websites and other media that are completely independent of the university – in a lot of cases these cause trouble and get up the noses of the university officials. The most famous and established of these 'independent' papers is *Cherwell* at Oxford University, which has been running since 1920 and has had a website since 1996 (in web terms that's pretty early). Some rather famous people and respected journalists have moved through its ranks, including media mogul Rupert Murdoch, BBC TV news presenter Peter Sissons and author Graham Greene.

Other publications independent from their students' unions include *Varsity* (Cambridge), *The Soton Tab* (Southampton), *The Linc* (Lincoln), *Palatinate* (Durham) and *The Founder* (Royal Holloway).

But you don't want to simply get involved with student media – you want to make it count! Here are five tips for making the most out of your student media days:

1 **Try everything** There are so many skills to pick up in student media and so many opportunities going – there can never be too many people working for a student paper, for example. So as well as being a sports reporter, do some proof-reading. Think you're a serious news editor? Make sure you do some podcasting too. Don't miss out on anything.

2 **Be bold** When you're on work experience, or even later in a job, you'll be bottom of the pile and doing as you're told. But being involved in student media you can be the boss, and when you are – take risks and make mistakes. It's the best way to learn.

3 **Collect contacts** You might think that being involved in student media is unimpressive, but the reputation of your student media outlet is likely to be able to open doors for you. Make sure you use it to bag big-name interviews, get your foot into exclusive events and build up a wealth of media (and other) contacts, from organisations to PR companies. Once you've wowed them with your professionalism, they may become a contact for your future career (or even be the door-opener to it).

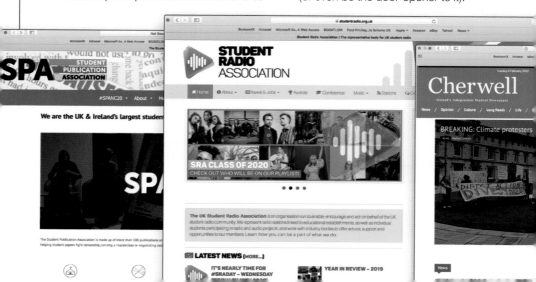

SOME USEFUL RESOURCES TO HELP KICK-START YOUR MEDIA CAREER

- **STUDENT RADIO ASSOCIATION** – This is the national association for all the student radio stations in the UK. Find out which are members and then learn about their yearly awards. www.studentradio.org.uk
- **NATIONAL STUDENT TELEVISION ASSOCIATION (NaSTA)** – The national association for all the student television stations across the country. They also hold an awards ceremony. http://nasta.tv/
- **STUDENT PUBLICATION ASSOCIATION (SPA)** – Relatively new compared to the other associations (I was involved in the initial discussions about setting it up), the SPA represents student publications across the UK. It provides support and advice and holds a yearly conference. Its awards celebrate the best work each year. www.spajournalism.co.uk
- **JOURNO RESOURCES** – Started in 2016 by former SPA chair Jem Collins, this is an amazing site packed with job opportunities, graduate schemes, tips and advice to help you find your way into a journalism career. www.journoresources.org.uk

4 **Take it seriously** Yes, of course it's going to be a great laugh – working in the media at any level can be the best job in the world – but take it seriously. It's a great chance to learn the disciplines needed to be successful in your chosen field.

5 **Get online** An expansion of the first point, in that this is a chance to try everything. We all know journalism is becoming less about print, more about online, so this is your chance to try podcasting, video reports, live-blogging and much more – all of which you can do using free/very cheap programs. This applies to other areas as well. Get involved with posting your own videos online on YouTube or Vimeo, and for radio work get making your own podcasts. If you can graduate and go to an employer telling them how you've amassed a wide range of skills you'll immediately impress them.

University sport

According to British Universities & Colleges Sport (BUCS), the national governing body for higher education sport in the UK, more than 100,000 students regularly take part in competitions, leagues and events at university. BUCS itself organises sport for more than 170 universities and colleges, and over 4,800 teams take part in their competitions – that's a lot of sport!

Sports teams are organised and overseen by either the students union or an athletic union. But what is it that makes sport so popular? BUCS shared their thoughts:

Students are an undeniably sporty lot. The British Active Students Survey for the 2018/19 academic year found that 47.1% of female students and 43.5% of male students aged between 16 and 25 years old were "fairly active" exercising 31 to 149 minutes a week. 23.7% (female) and 35.6% of students took it to the next level keeping fit for over 150 minutes a week.

'Sport at university proves popular as it means that those who have enjoyed the sporting offer at school or college can continue to play sport with like-minded individuals. The opportunity to play competitive sport and represent one's university in the BUCS leagues and Championships again has a strong appeal for a specific group of students. For those that enjoy activity and sport but failed to find the right sporting offer at school or college, university offers a wider range of sporting opportunities alongside the more typical sports offer, such as rugby, football, hockey, athletics and cricket. Sports such as lacrosse and Ultimate Frisbee present new and exciting sporting offers and BUCS has measured large-scale growth in these sports in Higher Education.

Whether you play competitive sport for your university, on an intra mural level or simply are looking to participate in some sort of physical activity, sport at university provides a great way to socialise and build new friendships and friendship groups with like-minded individuals outside academic pathways.'

Getting involved in university sport can play a large part in making your university experience better. It is a great way to make friends and gives you a sense of being part of something bigger. It also helps to add an extra level of structure to your life – getting to training sessions, matches, tournaments and other team events will require you to organise your time, which can motivate you to keep on top of other aspects of uni, like that all-important work.

Also, when you're away from home, staying healthy isn't always at the top of the student agenda – healthy eating goes out the window and this, coupled with the countless drinking benders, means that keeping in shape can be a bit of a chore. Obviously, playing sport at university is a counter to the inevitable excesses of student life – it is fun and regular exercise. What's more, better health means a more productive version of you, which can only be a good thing.

BUCS sum up some of the many benefits of getting involved:

'The benefits of sport and a healthy lifestyle are well documented and not specific to those undertaking sport at university.

Perhaps some focus should be placed on the benefits of sport in the eyes of potential employers and the personal development that sport provides. Employers cite individuals who have played or been involved with sport as having skills that possibly others have not developed. Leadership, teamwork, self-motivation alongside skills that may come with helping to run a sports club all help to build a real case for employment.'

And university sport doesn't just impact on student life; the skills and talent that are honed on our campuses feed through into professional sport. BUCS again: 'Student athletes have a much greater impact on the Olympic programme than what might be described as professional sport. HE and those going through the BUCS sporting offer have contributed significantly to Team GB over the course of history and in recent times over 50 per cent of Team GB has been made up of those currently or those having passed through higher education.'

The undisputed top university for sporting achievement in the UK is Loughborough. As well as being a force to reckon with across all sports, they have an illustrious history of churning out sporting greats. You may even recognise some of the names who studied there – such as Olympic bid leader and gold medallist Sebastian Coe, javelin legend Steve Backley, and Baroness Tanni Grey-Thompson, Paralympian. According to their website, 85 students, alumni and Loughborough-based athletes were selected for the Rio 2016 Olympic or Paralympic Games. So, you can see that even if you aren't quite at Olympic standard, getting involved in organised sport at university can only be of benefit.

Travel

What with all that hard study there's a good chance you might want to get away from it all for a bit. You don't have a great deal of money, but if planned right there are still plenty of amazing places you can visit on your student budget. Here I'll look at a few good options for student getaways, and how to stay safe when you're there.

Where to go?

Need some inspiration about where to go with your limited cash? Take a look at the suggestions on the next few pages for some great student breaks. When you're deciding where to go, think about how much it's going to cost to eat and sleep when you get there. You might find a really cheap flight to Iceland, for example, but check out how much a beer or a taxi fare is there – you'll very quickly lose the advantage of bargain air fares.

STUDENT TRAVEL CARDS

As with everything else, as a student you can get some pretty sweet discounts on travel. Here are some of the cards you can get your mitts on:

16–25 YOUNG PERSONS RAILCARD

With this card save ⅓ off rail fares across the UK. It costs just £28 for one year or £65 for three years. You can get one if you're between 16 and 25, or over 26 and in full-time education.
www.16-25railcard.co.uk

YOUNG PERSONS COACHCARD

Much the same as the railcard, this card gives you cheap coach tickets with a saving of up to 30%. As long as you're aged between 16 and 26, or a full time student you are eligible.
www.nationalexpress.com/coach/offers/studentcoachdeals.aspx

18+ OYSTER CARD

If you are studying in London you are entitled to nice discounts on your Oyster card (the London travel card). This will give you 30% off the standard adult travel card prices.
www.tfl.gov.uk/tickets/14312.aspx

ISIC CARD

With the International Student Identity Card (ISIC) you can get thousands of travel, online and lifestyle discounts in over 100 countries worldwide. With an additional free global roaming SIM card you can save up to 70% on using your phone abroad. All this and it is just £9.
www.isic.org

Barcelona, Spain

Spain is very popular with students, and there's a reason that Barcelona tops the list: it's basically an awesome place to visit. Whether you're planning to go for one of the city's music festivals, like Primavera or Sonar, or you just want an exciting place that gives you a little bit of everything, Barcelona is it. It has a great selection of art, culture and nightlife, alongside a gorgeous coastline and great beaches.

FIVE THINGS TO SEE AND DO IN BARCELONA

1 **Barcelona FC museum** An obvious must-see in the city, especially if you're a footie fan. Covering the history of one of Europe's most prestigious clubs, it has wall-to-wall trophies, statues of team greats and pictures. You can get a ticket to see the museum and a visit inside the legendary Camp Nou stadium or a special ticket which involves the museum and a behind-the-scenes look at the club, including visiting the changing rooms, VIP lounge and press conference areas.

2 **Sagrada Familia** This unfinished temple, designed by master architect Antonio Gaudi, is easily one of the city's most famous landmarks. It's been under construction since 1882 but is nearing completion depending on funding and resources. It's still magnificent and worth a visit.

3 **Las Ramblas** Las Ramblas (or the Rambles) is the pedestrian walkway that cuts from the city centre right down to the beach and waterfront. Teeming with life, it has market stalls and entertainers and is full of bars and cafes. You might want to avoid eating and drinking here, due to the massively inflated prices, but walking its length is certainly something that has to be done on any visit to Barcelona.

4 **Parc d'Atracciones del Tibidabo** Made famous in the Woody Allen movie *Vicky Cristina Barcelona*, Tibidabo Amusement Park is a stunning hundred-year-old antique amusement park on top of Tibidabo Hill. The park overlooks the city of Barcelona, towards the sea, so also offers amazing views.

5 **Park Güell** This interesting park was intended to be a stylish place for the Barcelona elite to hang out and is another design by celebrated architect Antonio Gaudi. The place is a showcase of Gaudi's eccentric style, containing amazing stone structures, stunning artistic tiling and weird buildings – it's a truly different place to hang out. At the entrance to the park is one of Gaudi's houses, which is now a museum.

Amsterdam, Netherlands

Amsterdam is popular with some people for the obvious reasons, but it's also a vibrant small city that has a lot to offer (yes, much more than the red light district and those 'coffee shops'). It's a beautiful city situated on a grid of stunning canals, with an excellent artistic heritage and the obvious amazing nightlife. It's a perfect place to visit whether you want a crazy or a more refined trip.

FIVE THINGS TO SEE AND DO IN AMSTERDAM

1. **Heineken Experience** If you're partial to an ice-cold lager, this is one of the must-see attractions in Amsterdam. Find out the history of the Heineken family and see how the beer is made before trying out some free samples. The lager really does taste better in its home town! Two drinks are included in the price of the ticket, and an extra one is available at a tasting bar.

2. **De Negen Straatjes** A vibrant neighbourhood of 'nine little streets', full of quirky stores selling everything from clothing and books to art and food. Visit it for a true sense of shopping in bohemian Amsterdam, and for things a little bit out of the ordinary.

3. **Red light district** This is obviously something that the Dutch city is famous for, and really is the most obvious evidence of their liberal lifestyle and culture. You might think that this doesn't appeal but it's worth visiting to get a good view of how differently sex is viewed in Holland. It's astonishing to see all walks of human life in one place. To see women with children walking past prostitutes in windows is initially a bit strange, but it isn't seen as shocking – everyone lives together just fine. Although it's obviously more open (and seedier) than life in Britain, it is, mostly, harmless. It might not be your bag but it's a must-see in Amsterdam.

4. **Sexmuseum Amsterdam Venustempel** Yes, it is a museum of sex. It's worth a visit for a few laughs and is actually fascinating. Obviously, give this place a miss if sex and flesh offend you.

5. **Anne Frankhuis (Anne Frank House)** This is the house where Anne Frank wrote what is probably the world's most famous diary. During the German occupation of the city in World War Two Frank lived in secret in the back of her father's office building, until she and her family were betrayed to the Nazis. It's a fascinating, eye-opening and eerie place to visit and a very real reminder of what Jews went through in Nazi Europe.

Saint Petersburg, Russia

This might not be top of your list for a visit, but Saint Petersburg offers something very different. Experience its clash of history, Soviet and Western culture. It's a city steeped in culture and there's a high chance of having some of the most unusual experiences of your life – great nightlife in a great city with a talent for the bizarre! Plus currently the Russian National Tourism Office is offering inexpensive bespoke packages for just a few hundred pounds all-in.

FIVE THINGS TO SEE AND DO IN SAINT PETERSBURG

1 **Purga** This is a pretty stereotypical basement bar (apart from the puppets having sex and the giant pirate's head on the wall ...). Here locals celebrate New Year every night, dancing to a strange mixture of '90s dance hits and Russian pop ditties. It's well worth joining the drunken revellers for a party that inexplicably involves everyone wearing bunny ears.

2 **Yusupov Palace** Saint Petersburg has hundreds of palaces. This one on the Moika River is magnificent and contains some of Europe's most interesting history. It's the building where Grigory Rasputin (the notorious 'Mad Monk') was murdered in 1916. The story of his death is worth hearing in the room where the plot to kill him unfolded. Elsewhere in the palace the breathtaking private theatre is as beautiful as it is surprising, and one of the most amazing rooms in the world. It's an absolute must-see.

3 **Hermitage Museum** Recognised as the second largest museum in the world, the Hermitage Museum houses a gigantic art collection within the lavish interiors of the former imperial residence. It contains a mind-blowing 2.7 million exhibits, which, it's claimed, would take you nine years to view if you looked at each exhibit for just one minute!

4 **Tinkoff Brewery** Why not sample some local beer in this old brewery, which is today a modern, sophisticated drinking den. You can easily enjoy a chat while sampling a tasty local beverage. Beers come in one-litre glasses, so you get plenty of booze for your bucks.

5 **Grand Palace Peterhof (or Catherine Palace)** This palace is an ornate wonder sat in the middle of huge, beautiful gardens, and is a beacon of wealth that shows just why it all ended in a revolution. Captured and burned down by the Nazis in World War Two, the palace is some way through a long-term restoration project to restore it to its former glory, and is a magnificent place to visit.

Dublin, Ireland

When looking for a break, don't discount the Emerald Isle just west of the UK! Dublin is a top destination, especially when it's St Patrick's Day (a great excuse for a mid-March mini-break). There are loads of student discounts, with free entry to some of the most popular sights, plus a vibrant club and bar scene. Make sure you check out what discounts and events are on offer before you leave.

FIVE THINGS TO SEE AND DO IN DUBLIN

1 **Guinness Storehouse** Have a little think. What's the one thing you associate with Ireland more than anything else? It's Guinness, isn't it? So visiting this former brewery is a must. It's now a large-scale exhibition covering everything you need to know about the black stuff. The section on the memorable Guinness advertising campaigns throughout the years is extremely entertaining. It's a bit pricey to get in, but it does come with a pint in the circular, glass-walled, rooftop Gravity Bar.

2 **Kilmainham Gaol** Visit one of Europe's most notorious prisons, where the leaders of the 1916 uprising were executed. The cold and bare cells have been maintained in perfect order. These days tours tend to focus more on the events of 1916 than anything else.

3 **Dublin Zoo** The city's zoo has a wonderful array of wildlife, and who doesn't love animals? It has 'African Plains', home to zebras, hippos, rhinos, lions, cheetahs, giraffes and chimps, plus 'World of Cats', 'World of Primates' and 'Fringes of the Arctic'. There's a creature for everyone!

4 **Temple Bar** This area, with its preserved medieval street pattern and narrow cobbled streets, has been dubbed 'Dublin's cultural quarter'. It's a lively area full of pubs and bars and is the perfect place for a night out. During the day it's a bit of a shoppers' paradise and at night it's party central.

5 **Saint Patrick's Cathedral** The Catholic faith is central to Ireland's past and present. Saint Patrick's Cathedral is said to be the oldest Christian site in the country. It's also the largest, and one of the most visited places in Dublin.

Berlin, Germany

First and foremost Berlin is pretty much considered Europe's most cutting-edge city for clubbing, with a massive techno and underground dance scene. It's also pretty decent for sightseeing. It's a huge city that has loads of places to explore, and famous landmarks to photograph.

FIVE THINGS TO SEE AND DO IN BERLIN

1 **Topography of Terror** Nazi Germany could be a scary place to live. The Secret State Police and the SS reigned with a rule of terror. There's now a permanent exhibition showing the terror of the Third Reich on the site where the headquarters of the Secret State Police, the SS and the Reich Security Main Office were located.

2 **Berlin Wall** The most infamous symbol of the cold war era, and one that split Berliners for decades. Unfortunately, as a tourist attraction only a few sections of the wall remain, but they're still well worth a visit. Some exist with original watchtowers intact but more are expected to disappear over the next few years.

3 **Watergate** One of the coolest clubs in a city of cool clubs. On two levels, the club's spectacular lower dance floor, called 'Waterfloor', overlooks the River Spree through a huge ceiling-to-floor glass front, and has an illuminated bridge – it's said that it's like you're dancing on water. It boasts a fine array of international DJs playing house and drum and bass. In summer you can dance on the outside deck by the river.

4 **Checkpoint Charlie** Probably the most poignant reminder of Berlin's turbulent recent past, Checkpoint Charlie was the infamous border between East and West Berlin (between capitalism and communism). After 13 August 1961 this was the only place tourists, military personnel and diplomats from the West could enter the Communist state. A section of the Berlin Wall has been rebuilt near the checkpoint. It's a must-see sight in Berlin and historically fascinating.

5 **Tiergarten** The city's largest park is fantastic to walk around, and also contains some of Berlin's other main attractions including Berlin Zoo and Aquarium, which houses over 13,000 animals.

Tenerife, Canary Islands

With the number of deals available on trips to the Canary Islands they're a popular choice when the weather in the UK is miserable. Tenerife is known as 'the island of eternal spring', which means exactly what is suggests – gorgeous weather. It's also famous for its stunning beaches and lively nightlife. If you're interested in outdoor activities you'll find plenty of things to do, from hiking to scuba diving. And if you're feeling really adventurous, hop on a ferry to see one of the other seven islands in the Canaries.

FIVE THINGS TO SEE AND DO IN TENERIFE

1 **Siam Park** This is a kick-ass water park. In fact it's considered one of the best in the world. Whether you want to kick back and relax or get your adrenaline pumping, it has everything you need for your own water-based adventure.

2 **Teide National Park** Like visiting another planet, this volcanic wonderland is well worth a visit. Out of its centre rises Mount Teide, an active volcano and the highest peak in Spain. It's so amazing that it's been used in many films, including the remake of *Clash of the Titans* in 2010.

3 **Tenerife Zoo Monkey Park** Everyone likes monkeys, right? This place has lots of them, and you can feed them too. Visit for some monkey magic.

4 **Playa de las Americas (The Patch)** Looking for somewhere to eat and drink? The Patch has loads of places to satisfy your hunger and thirst.

5 **Palm Beach Surf School** Learn to surf in a place with perfect conditions for surfing. The accredited instructors are with you in the water every step of the way, so it's a safe way to get to grips with the sport.

Malta

This Mediterranean island is an increasingly popular destination for students, with an ever-improving club scene that's starting to rival dance mecca Ibiza in a big way. You'll find a good mix of excursions too, with beautiful historical sites as well as rock climbing, wind surfing and more. It's a small island, so you can start a day of sightseeing with a swim, and relax on the beach before getting ready for an evening out.

FIVE THINGS TO SEE AND DO IN MALTA

1 **Chamber of Secrets** No, this isn't a Harry Potter themed joint, but it won't disappoint! It's a dinner theatre show with traditional Maltese cuisine and comedy, singing, magic and other illusions. It is a top night out and a little different from the usual nightclubs.

2 **Malta Music Week** If you want to hear some fine tunes, Malta Music Week (which takes place in June each year) is a good time to go. Big names play throughout the week in stunning locations.

3 **Diving Malta** If you have a sense of adventure, diving in Malta is definitely something you should give a go. The stunning Maltese waters are suitable for beginners and pros alike.

4 **Mdina Old City** One of Europe's finest examples of an ancient walled city. Walking through the narrow paved streets is like walking back through history.

5 **Gianpula** Malta's largest open-air club, Gianpula hosts five different areas – The Main Room, Molecule, Marrakech, Groove Gardens and Gianpula Fields – and its highlights include the garden and swimming pool. It hosts big names, the likes of Faithless, Timo Maas, Sasha and John Digweed all having played the venue.

Staying in hostels

As a student, no matter what you're doing on your travels, hostels are likely to be your home away from home. You've no doubt heard horror stories about some people's stays in hostels, but they really aren't all that bad, and some can be really nice. If all you're looking for is a clean place to sleep and shower, a little research beforehand can guarantee you get what you need.

If you're completely new to staying in hostels, here's some basic information and a few tips to get you started and make sure you get the best out of your hostel stay.

You probably know people who've been travelling before, maybe even to the place you're visiting. Ask them about which hostels or places to look for that they recommend, and also which they'd suggest you steer clear of.

Rooms in most hostels are split between private rooms and dormitories. Private rooms are, well, private. They're usually singles, twins or doubles, though some hostels also offer triples. Dorms vary in size, but range from four to twenty beds (or sometimes even more, especially in European cities). Most dorms will have rows of bunk beds, though some offer a selection of bunks and regular single or double beds.

A lot of hostels have a few en-suite

Travel safety tips

Before you head off on your trip there are a few things you'll need to know. Luckily there's a government website on hand to tell you most of them. Check it out here: www.fco.gov.uk/travel

The following are a few of the things you'll definitely need to consider before and during your travels:

- **Are you covered for injury and illness?** You need to make sure you're covered for this, as an emergency abroad can be seriously expensive. If you're not covered to get yourself fixed up abroad and need to be medically repatriated to the UK, this could cost thousands of pounds. An air ambulance from the Canary Islands, for instance, can cost up to £16,000 (figures supplied by FirstAssist Services Ltd).

  It's really important that you take out full travel insurance when you book your holiday, as this will cover you if for some reason you have to cancel, or the holiday firm goes bust. Make sure the cover you choose is appropriate for the trip you are taking – not only the destination, but also any activities you may do (skiing, skydiving etc are not covered by a standard policy) and any special luggage or sporting equipment you may be taking.

  It's also a very good idea to check the Foreign Office website in advance if you are going somewhere that may potentially be dangerous, and keep an eye on the news. If the government advises that it is too dangerous to go somewhere, it would be sensible to take heed. It's better to lose money and the chance for an adventure than it is to lose your life.

  There are loads of websites and books devoted to travelling on a shoestring, and given that you'll have long holidays, you'll have time to explore alternative itineraries that may cost a lot less and take you off the beaten path. Remember, once you are in full-time work your holidays will be very limited, so use this time to explore the world. Stay safe and have fun!

- **Do you have the right currency?** You'll need money abroad, so find out what currency you're going to need and convert some pounds. While you'll probably be able to use your credit card in most places, it always helps to have cash for taxis, phone calls, snacks and impulse souvenir buys.

- **Can you communicate?** True, there are a lot of places where people will speak English (other countries are so much better at learning foreign tongues than us Brits), but you'll go far by knowing at least some basic phrases. You don't need to be fluent in the language, but knowing how to ask for help, how much something costs and where the toilets are will be very helpful.

rooms available, giving you even more privacy. Standard rooms mean sharing communal showers and toilets with everyone else in the hostel.

Many hostels have a kitchen where you can cook your own meals, and some have restaurants, cafes and bars. Most offer lockers (either free or for a small cost) to help secure your valuables.

A few hostels have curfews or lock-outs, though this isn't very common. It's worth checking this before you book – the last thing you want is to find yourself locked out at 2:00am.

Also check the hostel's website to see if bed linen is provided. Sheets usually will

be, as this helps to cut down on bedbug problems from dirty sleeping bags, but you'll probably either have to hire towels or bring your own.

Signing up for a Hostelling International membership will give you savings across all the hostel associations worldwide, saving you a few quid on your travels and your accommodation. Visit www.hihostels.com to find out more.

Also, by at least attempting to speak in their language people will probably be happier to help you out.

- **Do you have a plan?** While not knowing what the next day will hold is part of the fun of travelling, you should have some basic plans in mind and have a rough idea of how to get around the place you're staying. Get a decent travel guide, and make sure you have a map. Lost tourists are an easy target for pickpockets and con artists, so make sure you know where you're going.

- **Do you know the laws?** There are certain things that are as illegal everywhere else as they are over here, but it's worth knowing what you can and can't do in the places you're visiting. Laws aren't the same everywhere, and punishments can be a lot more severe than here for crimes like drug use or disorderly behaviour. The last holiday memory you want is to be stuck in some grotty foreign prison.

- **Do you know where your bag is?** Hold on to your bags all the time, and don't carry your passport and all your valuables with you if you don't need to. Since the 9/11 attacks the authorities everywhere have become even jumpier about unattended bags, and the last thing you want to do is cause an unnecessary terror threat.
  On a more personal note, it's very easy to

have your stuff nicked on public transport or in a crowd of people; don't make it easy for someone to swipe all your valuables in one go.

- **Have you secured the valuables you have left behind?** If you've left anything in your room, have you made sure it's secure? If your room or the hotel has a safe, lock your most important valuables in it. If you're staying in a multi-bed room in a hostel it's not a bad idea to lock your suitcase or bag in a safe overnight – you never know who's about.

- **Is everything in your bag yours?** Has someone you've just met on holiday asked you to carry something in your bag before boarding a plane? Don't do it! – not even if you think you can trust them. Carrying drugs and other contraband out of foreign countries is big business and can result in some seriously severe punishments. Under the law it's your bag, so it's your responsibility.

- **Who do you call?** Have the numbers of your bank, mobile phone provider, credit card company and the local British consulate in case you do have your wallet, passport or phone stolen. It'll save you an Internet search (which can cost you money as well). Remember to add +44 to any numbers you're calling in the UK.

Chapter 7
Study

It might come as a bit of a shock to you, but at university you also have to do some studying. It's easy to joke about it, but quite a few students simply forget to do this. I know it's the boring bit of university life, but the tips in this chapter will help make it as painless as possible for you to get some top marks.

What are lecturers looking for?

No matter what you do, or how strict the marking criteria is, the fact remains that the mark you get depends quite a bit on what the person marking it is looking for.

To get a bit of insight into this I asked a few lecturers around the country for some tips and pointers to help you lot get the best marks possible:

'Instead of the essay being applied to the text, the text – its language, its ideas, its images, its "feel" (to use an old-fashioned word) – will seep into your writing. A reader can always tell if an essay grows out of the text or is simply an exercise. But there are various ways of writing an essay: some students plan by making lists of details in a text, some use diagrams, but one way is to take it in stages. I propose four stages – examining the question, selecting your quotations, organising your notes and readings, and writing your work.' – Martin Coyle, Professor and Head of English Literature at the School of English Communication and Philosophy, Cardiff University.

'Clarity, succinctness, and intelligence. Work needs to be refreshing and insightful, with a strong sense of stylistic air. Work that's easy to read, in terms of style, grammar and structure, is always graded higher, as it makes reading the work a pleasure not a chore. Background knowledge that shows depth and understanding of the subject will go a long way in scoring higher grades, and most of all it needs to read as if you enjoyed writing it, because if you enjoy writing your work, often (but not always) the reader will enjoy reading it.' – João Rodrigues, University of Coimbra, Portugal.

> ## Work needs to be refreshing and insightful, with a strong sense of stylistic air.

Assorted lecturers at the University of Bristol got together and chose these two points:

1 **Original thought.** The key to being awarded high marks is to demonstrate original thought. That is to say that students must not only respond to a question or engage with a theory, but must do so in a way that illustrates a level of understanding that goes above and beyond what's been covered in the curriculum. Students must show that they've researched more than what's directly required by the question in order to form their own opinions and points of view on the topic being covered.

2 **Engagement with critical theory.** Students must be able to confidently handle both primary and secondary sources within a wider discussion, locating the topics of their discussion within a wider framework of critical theory.

Planning

You probably want to get your university work done as quickly and with as little effort as possible – planning might therefore sound like too much extra work. But with just a little bit of preparation you can make completing your university work much quicker and much more effective. Use these tips to get the most out of your academic planning:

Know your deadlines

Knowing what needs to be done and when for is key to good planning. There's no point reading for an essay that needs to be in after an important presentation if you haven't done enough for that! Start your term's planning by noting down all your deadlines and then work the rest of your plans outwards from that.

Plan your time

This doesn't mean planning every second of every day but draw up a simple list of tasks to complete each day, to help keep on top of things. With technology there are plenty of apps available to help you do this, and if you are using an email program such as Microsoft Outlook you can plan your diary in that, setting tasks and to-do lists.

Write out your plan of attack

One of the main hurdles in completing academic work is figuring out how to get from A to B. A – simply having the full details of the assignment and B – completing it successfully. Write out a plan of the stages you need to go through to get to the end.

- **Break it down** To help get your plan of attack together, break the main question down into smaller questions that need to be answered. Work your way outwards from each question to determine what you need to do and what resources you need in order to answer each question. Breaking it down like this will make the whole task seem less daunting and make it easier to get started.

- **Change is good: redraft and amend** Just because you have a plan it doesn't mean it has to stay the same throughout the project. As you do more reading, and uncover more points to be addressed or answered, amend and redraft your plan to take this into account. Plans are there to make sure that you have goals to help you complete the work, but it's also important to be flexible in regard to changing them.

- **Stick to the plan** Considering the last point this might sound like a bit of a contradiction, but while the individual aspects of the plan can, and should, change as the work progresses, the whole point of creating a plan in the first place is to give you something to work to. So stick to your timeframes, to-do lists and goals. Ignoring your plan will mean that the work spent creating it was a waste of time!

Presentations

It's likely that doing presentations will form part of your course. These can be nerve-wracking ordeals if you're not ready for them, but with a bit of preparation and practice there's absolutely no reason why you shouldn't nail every presentation put in your way.

As with all academic work, preparation is the key. When starting your presentation work there are a few things you need to consider:

■ **Who are your audience?** What are they likely to know already? Do they all have to produce the same presentation as you?

■ **How long is the presentation expected to be?** The length of the presentation will make a huge difference to how much information you should and can include.

■ **What are your aims, topics and goals?** What do you need to cover in your presentation, and what do you hope to have shown or proved by the end of it? Understanding this at the start will make preparation much easier.

■ **Have you ordered your thoughts?** Once you've collected your research it's a good plan to arrange your ideas in the sequence in which you want to raise them. This is a simple way to get some structure into your topic.

■ **Does it fit an established presentation structure?** I'd recommend writing your presentation in the following way:

1 **Introduction** – Introduce the topic and what you're going to discuss.
2 **Main body** – Discuss your research and make your main points.
3 **Conclusions** – Summarise the points you've made and what conclusions you've come to.

■ **Have you backed up all your points?** Make sure that all the points you make are backed up by supporting evidence, and that all the facts you've used have been checked to be correct.

■ **Are your key points highlighted?** If you're going to use notes or key words during your presentation, make sure they're reduced to succinct bullet-points and word lists. This will help you keep your presentation flowing. Also maintain as much eye contact with the audience as possible.

Preparing visual aids

As exciting as you might think the sound of your voice is, it will really help your presentation to back it up with some visual aids. This will make it much more accessible and engaging to your audience, and will score you a few more marks.

These days technology can once again come to the rescue – no projectors and acetate sheets any more! There are various bits of software you can use to produce your visual presentation, the most common being Microsoft Powerpoint or Google Slides.

Practice

You know what they say, 'practice makes perfect', and it's the same with presentations. The better you know it, the better your delivery will be on the day. Follow these steps to make sure you're fully prepared:

- **Delivery** So you've planned and practised as much as you can for the presentation and now it's the big day. It would be a shame to blow everything at the last hurdle, but there's still plenty that can go wrong. But if you take your time, relax and follow these simple pointers you should waltz through it.
- **Look the part** There's no need to overdo the smartness of your dress but you should at least dress tidily enough to show you mean business. That means no ripped jeans, dirty trainers and unwashed T-shirts.
- **At the start of the presentation greet the audience** This will make them feel part of the proceedings and warm them to you (and remember to keep that eye-contact).
- **Try to look confident and relaxed**... even if inside you're almost crippled with stage-fright! Also try to smile.

- **Don't rush** It might seem tempting to bang through it all at breakneck speed, but take your time to ensure you get your points across clearly. It'll also make it easier to stay in control and not panic.
- **Stand to either side of the screen** Don't stand in front of your visual aids.
- **Make good use of the visual aids** Try to refer to and point out the visual aids that support the point you're making. This will add another level to the explanation you're giving and make the presentation more accessible to the audience.
- **If you get stressed...** Take deep breaths and use natural pauses in your speech to get back in control. This works extremely well. People might not even notice that you're stressed.
- **Use your voice to make points** Change the volume and tone of your voice and use pauses to differentiate between points and emphasise the most important ones.
- **Conclude by summarising the main points** Depending on how long your presentation has been it's likely people will have had a lot of information to take on board. Summarise the things you most want them to remember and display them as bullet points as you go through them.
- **Answer questions simply and directly** This will make you appear confident and have a solid grasp of the subject matter.

WHAT TO DO IN YOUR VISUAL PRESENTATION

- Highlight only the key points from your presentation as bullet points, or in a similarly accessible format. Make these the bits of information that you most want your audience to take away with them.
- Use a font size that's easy for the whole audience to read.
- Make sure that all the pictures and diagrams used are also easily viewable by the audience in terms of size and quality.
- Don't clutter the slides or pages in your presentation. Keep it clean and simple to read – it's better to use more slides or pages than to cram it all into a few.
- Be careful with your use of colour. Sure, that funky green background might look nice, but can the audience still read the text, and does it overwhelm the diagrams you're using? It's worth thinking about these things when planning your presentation.
- Read and learn your presentation. Get it etched into your brain.
- Rehearse it out loud as if you're delivering it to an audience.
- Try and have a dry run with friends to gauge their reaction.
- Time your rehearsals to make sure you're within the time-limit for the presentation.
- If you're using notes, practise with them to ensure you deliver everything as smoothly as possible.
- Anticipate the kind of questions you might be asked afterwards, and have some idea of the answers you might give.

Your dissertation

If there's one word that's enough to send most students into a blind panic it's 'dissertation'. It's the biggie, the daddy of all your university work and the one piece that shows your academic prowess. It's the most important piece of work of your university life and it can seem like an insurmountable and daunting task.

But you do have a long while to do it, and with a little bit of preparation and decent planning you can easily find yourself on the road to dissertation success.

Here are the top ten tips to help you stay on top of your dissertation:

1 **Start early** Start on the work as soon as you can. If you use all the time available you should be able to produce a gleaming gem of a dissertation. It really is much easier to do a dissertation in six months than it is in six days.

2 **Keep a diary** You can use a traditional diary, or make use of a digital diary and task list using a program like Microsoft Outlook – this can help you set goals, keep track of your progress and help you manage your time. It will also allow you to set reminders to keep you focussed on tasks. Plan each month in advance. Just don't get too stuck in timetables.

3 **Set your own personal deadlines** Yes, I know the university have set you deadlines, but to help you hit those it's a good idea for you to set your own, based on your personal working style, skills and time restrictions. Planning this will help you keep on top of your workload and other life commitments.

4 **Only take out five books at a time** The human brain is an impressive thing, but it can't deal with 40 books all at the same time. Don't try and cram it all in all at once, apply method to the madness

and approach your reading one section (or point) at a time.

5 **Keep a running bibliography and list of references** Make life easy on yourself. It is a real headache trying to add all the books and sources you've used right at the end. You will miss some, and you'll lose marks. In fact, if you use someone's ideas without properly referencing them you could find yourself hauled up for plagiarism. Add them as you go along so that you can keep on top of everything you've used.

6 **Use reading strategies** They may sound like academic hokum, but they really do help. They can help make reading a whole book in one sitting much more manageable, and in the long run can save you time and effort. Find one that suits you and use it to your advantage.

Reading strategies include skimming a text to get the gist, highlighting and annotating as you go along, drawing a map of the relevant concepts and ideas, and finally, summarising the text in your own words.

You will have a lot of reading to do, and you need to get the most out of it quickly and efficiently. Reading strategies give you a process to get maximum benefit from your reading with minimum effort.

7 **Always be prepared for dissertation meetings** These meetings are there to help you, so always have work prepared to show and discuss. Have questions to ask, especially if there are points you're unclear on – if you don't ask

the questions you'll never get the answers.

8 **Keep on top of the news** Make sure you keep on top of the latest news and happenings about your topic. This maximises your vocabulary and adds scope to what you can bring to a debate. Plus you don't want to make a point only to find out it was proven wrong while you were writing.

9 **Proofread more than once** Make sure you check your work over several times and ask others to read it over too. This will minimise the chance of mistakes being left in the final version. Mistakes mean lower marks.

10 **Keep an eye on presentation** Watch out for consistency of grammar and fonts etc, and make sure you're aware of the university's specific presentation requirements. Marks can be lost for using the wrong font and having the wrong line-spacing and borders – it's harsh but true. Don't panic and have to change lots at the last minute. Finishing touches could make a huge difference to your final grade so make time for the small stuff.

Problems with the Internet

Before the Internet, researching for academic work was a real pain. All you had was a library full of books and journals to sift through to get what you want. No Google, no online journals, no instant access to thousands of relevant pieces of work.

But while it does make life a lot easier, using the Internet for your uni work does have its own pitfalls. The main problem is that it's open to everyone, which means that anyone can publish information on the web about any topic. No one's watching what's put up and there's no quality control, which means there are a number of things that can be wrong with information available on the Internet. Remember that anything online could be:

■ **Out of date** Once something is on the Internet it's very likely it will be there forever. This means that the information may not have been updated and could be seriously out of date.

■ **Biased** With no quality control there's nothing stopping people publishing work written from a biased or distorted viewpoint, which in turn could give you an incorrect slant in your own work.

■ **Just wrong** There's absolutely nothing stopping people publishing things that simply aren't true! Obviously, using this stuff will lose you some serious marks.

■ **Commercial** A company could have paid to have an article published, or else published information to sell or show their products in a certain light, especially if there's been some controversy about them. This kind of material is unlikely to offer an objective and useful take on a subject.

One thing the Internet has created amongst students is a cut-and-paste culture to complete work. Why bother writing your own stuff when you can just copy and re-word someone else's? The problem is that universities have got pretty sophisticated at finding out who's nicking other people's work and trying to pass it off as their own – there's even software that can catch you out! Even if you didn't mean to do it you need to make sure you've referenced and logged the sources correctly so that it doesn't look like you're trying to cheat. Remember, if you can easily find a source online to cheat with, your lecturer can find the same thing just as easily. Plagiarism is a very serious issue at uni and it's best not to get caught doing it!

How to use the Internet properly for university work

Despite the problems, used properly the Internet is the best tool ever for getting top marks on your academic work. Seriously, you probably don't realise how lucky you are to have access to that amount of information at the touch of a button.

USE ACADEMIC SEARCH ENGINES AND GATEWAYS

Luckily some nice people have gone and done some of the work for you by creating academic search engines and gateways. For example, Google Scholar is just like normal Google but for academic information

sources, which means you're definitely using credible sources. Academic gateways are great sources of quality-checked resources. They're usually carefully selected sites sorted into specific subject areas. Ask your university which academic gateways they recommend using.

CHECK YOUR SOURCES

It's really important to check that your sources are reliable, up-to-date and relevant for your work. Check the source you're using with other relevant academic sources like research journals. Remember that some of the stuff on the Internet can be deceptive – it might look like a reputable academic source but is actually completely false.

THINGS TO CONSIDER WHEN YOU FIND INFORMATION ON THE INTERNET

- Who's the writer? Are they a recognised expert in the field? Is their name given, and what are their credentials?
- Who was it written for? Was it written for an academic audience, general readers, or people who already agree with the writer?
- Is it academic material and are references given?
- Is it biased? Is the writer trying to convince you of a particular viewpoint?
- Does the writer belong to an organisation with an interest in presenting a certain viewpoint?
- When was the information written?
- Does it properly reference the sources used?

If an Internet source uses other sources as reference points make sure you've cited both. All sources used must be cited at the relevant point in your work, and also in the bibliography or list of references.

Plagiarism

You'll hear this word mentioned a lot at university. Plagiarism is pretty much top of the naughty list in terms of academic crimes. And it's very serious, so serious in fact that in extreme cases you could find yourself kicked out of university or totally failing your degree.

Put simply, plagiarism is cheating. It refers to someone trying to pass off someone else's ideas as their own. At university this is not seen as 'borrowing', it's seen as stealing – and stealing is taken very seriously indeed.

If you don't own authorship of the work and don't clearly show who does, that's cheating. If you don't properly acknowledge the source of the information it's considered intellectual theft (or plagiarism).

At university as many cases of plagiarism are caused by misunderstanding as by people trying to cheat. Being a little uncertain or confused about exactly what to do regarding academic work may be a factor, but if so you really need to get clued up. Misunderstanding isn't accepted as an excuse for plagiarism. Get hold of your university's academic good practice guide, which should lead you through what's expected of you and what you need to do. It's best to start understanding this right from the beginning of your uni life.

Types of plagiarism

You'll be in big trouble if you're caught doing any of the following:

- **Trying to pass other people's work off as your own** You can't copy whole sentences and paragraphs and act like they're your own, even if you think that

> *If you don't own authorship of the work and don't clearly show who does, that's cheating.*

it's the best way to express the point you're trying to make and is better than you could ever do. Even if you have loads of your own notes taken from other sources and have forgotten to note where it came from, you can't use it. It's quite simple: using other people's words as your own is a big no-no.

- **Copying work but changing a few words or phrases** It's no good changing a few words and trying to pretend it's your work – it's still someone else's work and you need to credit them. You can paraphrase if you don't want to use full quotes.

- **Submitting the same work for different assignments** Yeah, people do this! Even if it is work for different departments, if you've been awarded marks for one piece of work you can't submit it again. It's cheating – it's like plagiarising yourself! Of course, you can use work from a past assignment if you credit the original source, even if the source is you!

And the university will catch you. When they do there really aren't that many excuses you can make – they've heard them all before. Here are just some of the most common reasons and excuses used to try and get away with it:

- Not understanding what plagiarism is.
- Having too much work to do and not having the time to submit original work.
- Not being very good at note-taking.
- Being under too much pressure to succeed (so they had to cheat).
- Having different academic values.
- Thinking it would be easy to get away with it.
- Instructions for the assignment weren't clear.
- Not having enough confidence to produce original work.
- Never having to acknowledge sources in work at school or college.

Needless to say, these excuses never work.

How will they catch you?

In the same way that the Internet has made it easier for people to cheat, it's made it easier for tutors to catch you doing it. Do you think that if you've easily found a source to steal from the university can't find that same source just as easily? If you do then you should probably give up university now, because you're clearly not very bright.

There are a number of ways you can be caught out:

- They can catch you with TurnitinUK online plagiarism detection software, which a lot of universities subscribe to. See, I told you technology also worked against you! Lecturers can log on to a vast database of previously submitted material, including student essays and assignments, over 12 billion websites, essays from cheat-sites (avoid these like the plague), databases and journals. If it's out there this thing will probably find it.
- Your tutors have a lot of experience and will have read a lot on the subject you're writing about. They'll probably know if you've copied sections of text from the recommended course reading list or from their lecture notes.
- Everyone has their own writing style, so if huge parts of your essay read differently it will set alarm bells ringing.
- If you all use the same books and sources and copy the best points your lecturer will notice straight away. This happens more than you might think.
- Back to cheat-sites again. There's a whole industry of dodgy sites offering bespoke essays to students at a price. Your university will be well aware of these sites and will know how to spot a cheat. You might get away with it, but there's a far higher chance that you'll get caught, in which case you'll lose the hundreds of pounds you gave to the cheats and also any chance of a grade on that essay. You may even lose your university place altogether. So I'll say it again – never use a cheat-site for your university work.
- Finally, probably the most obvious way, your lecturer can Google it. They can take the sentence, bang it in a search engine and see what comes up. If you've copied it you'll be caught straight away.

The only way not to get caught cheating is to understand what you need to do and not plagiarise other people's work. Simple as that.

Essay writing tips

Essay writing is pretty important for getting a degree, and it's something that a lot of people struggle with. The tips below aren't going to make it a doddle – you'll still have to put a lot of work in – but they will help you get the most out of your work and give you a chance of getting the marks.

■ **Use your time effectively** This is something that the majority of students don't do very well. Basically it means don't leave everything till the last minute. Make sure you schedule enough time for both the research and writing of the essay and stick to that schedule. Remember, a rushed essay won't be a good essay!

■ **Make sure you understand the topic or assignment** This probably sounds pretty patronising, but so many students fail their work simply because they don't understand what it is they were supposed to do. Don't be afraid to ask for advice from lecturers.

■ **Be organised** Make sure you're organised and plan what you need to do effectively. This includes managing your time, making structured essay plans and organising your research sources well. See the section on 'Planning' (page 138).

■ **Explore the question** Break down the question into smaller questions and answer each one. If this process raises more questions, answer them in turn, and follow this pattern until you're happy you have all the angles covered.

■ **Avoid plagiarism** It's that word again. It's being repeated because it's something you should avoid like the plague. It's important you don't steal other people's ideas and try to pass them off as your own. If you get caught not only will you fail but you'll more than likely be kicked out of uni.

■ **Keep checking your work** Are you keeping on topic? Are you still answering the question? Are you covering everything that needs to be covered? Does it make sense? Constantly checking these things will keep your writing focussed on the end goal.

■ **Leave it and come back** Once you've finished your essay, leave it and come back to it the next day with fresh eyes and re-read it. It might offer you a new perspective on what you've written and will probably help you improve it.

■ **Follow formatting** Your university will have provided you with some formatting guidelines for your essays – stick to them. Make sure you've used the correct font, text layout etc. Getting these wrong is a really stupid thing to be losing marks on.

■ **Get it checked by someone else** Have your work proofread by someone you trust. It's very hard to spot mistakes in your own work because you're too familiar with it. Fresh eyes will pick up mistakes you've missed and ensure that it all makes sense to someone coming to it cold.

■ **Stick to deadlines** This goes without saying. In most cases if you don't get an essay in on time, you've failed. No excuses, no chance to do it again, just a big, fat fail. Complete the essay the day before the hand-in date to give yourself the chance to make any changes, and allow yourself plenty of time to get it to the office.

■ **Learn from feedback** Take on board any notes your lecturer writes on your essay about why you lost marks and try to apply the advice to the next piece of work you do.

Postgraduate options

With the current state of the jobs market more and more students are taking their studies to postgraduate level (continuing academic life after getting an undergraduate degree). This will make you highly qualified and desirable to employers, so it might be a route you'll consider taking.

The majority of postgraduate study is independent. A few courses might incorporate a traditional teaching element, but most of the time it'll be down to you to set your own research aims and goals. Set tasks, guidelines and assignments are uncommon in postgraduate study.

Unlike any other type of study you'll have done, students are asked to come up with and develop ideas and theories that are entirely their own, and not learnt from other people's research.

The length of the course is also different to undergraduate study. Depending on the type of degree you take, postgraduate courses can be a lot shorter than undergraduate degrees, with many courses comprising just one year of full-time study. This means that postgraduate study is a lot more intense, requiring full focus and dedication to achieve a lot in a short period of time.

Types of postgraduate course
■ Postgraduate certificate
Postgraduate certificates aim to give you specialised knowledge over a full-time course that lasts between 9 and 12

- MA – master of arts.
- MSc – master of science.
- MBA – master of business administration.
- LLM – master of law.
- MEd – master of education.
- MPhil – master of philosophy.
- MRes – master of research.

The MBA is an international postgraduate business qualification that's respected by employers all over the world. Having one of these under your belt is seriously good for your CV.

There are also specialist postgraduate courses available for people seeking employment in specific areas of work. These are often similar to masters courses, but include taught theory alongside long placements. Often a research aspect will be incorporated as part of the course.

months. Your workload and the number of lectures you attend will vary massively depending on the type of course you take and which university or college you attend.

- **Postgraduate diploma** The work is much the same as for a postgraduate certificate but takes a shorter period of time, courses tending to last just a third of a year.
- **Research degree** On a research course you'll be asked to produce one (or more) pieces of original research. Exactly what this entails will depend on the subject you decide to study. The length of the course can also vary, from one to three (or more) years of full-time study.
- **Masters** Quite simply a Masters is for someone who's shown a 'mastery' of a specific subject or area of professional practice. It can be research-based, a taught course or a combination of both, and will take at least one year to complete. The workload will vary widely depending on the subject of study, and there's a chance you may have to submit a dissertation at the end of it.

- **Law courses** If you're looking to get into law you can study for the Graduate Diploma in Law (GDL) – occasionally referred to as the Common Professional Examination (CPE). This is a one-year course for those who haven't taken law as part of their undergraduate studies but want to practise law.

  To be a solicitor you need to take a one-year Legal Practice Course (LPC), whether you have an undergraduate law degree or a GDL. You need to take this before you can become a trainee solicitor. The Bar Vocational Course (BVC) is the equivalent course if you intend to be a barrister.

  The GDL, LPC, and BVC are all available as part-time courses spread over two years.
- **PGCE/PGDE** With fewer job prospects more and more graduates are choosing teaching as a career path. To do this you need to study for a qualification called a PGCE (Postgraduate Certificate in Education) in England, Wales and Northern Ireland, or a PGDE (Postgraduate Diploma in Education) elsewhere. Both usually last a year.

Chapter 8
Careers

Getting a better job is what you're at university for. Yes it is! And at the moment that's not as easy as it sounds; in fact it's harder than it's ever been. At present there are, on average, 75 people going for every graduate job, and that's serious competition. So if you want to be the one in 75 you need to know what you're doing when you go looking for a job. This chapter will give you a good starting point.

Work experience and internships

Because it's so hard to get a job at the moment you need to do everything you can to show employers that you're the best candidate, and little is better at doing that than getting some hands-on work experience.

It's no longer good enough just to wave your degree in an employer's face; nope, these people want actual experience. So, you can write about the job in an essay, but can you do it in practice?

Doing work experience will let you see what the job entails, and give you a nice easy step into the workplace. Carrying out duties or tasks that other employees do will allow you to see if you're good at it, and in some cases whether or not you actually want to do that kind of job.

Yes, in a lot of cases the stories of 'workies' just making tea and sorting post are true, but you'll at the very least get to see what the working environment is actually like.

You can do work experience at any point during your education, and it's well worth taking a week or two out. Basically, the more skills you acquire the better your CV will look.

Some courses include practical experience as part of the syllabus – these are called 'sandwich courses' because the work placement is like the filling in a three-year education sandwich. Whereas most work experience is voluntary and unpaid, placements as part of a sandwich course are usually paid because of their length (up to a year).

An internship is essentially a long period of work experience (anything from one week up to 12 months). You're expected to work much like one of the normal employees, but the focus is on you learning things and gaining skills for that job. There's currently a lot of controversy about companies exploiting young people with long, unpaid internships, with students being used like normal workers without being paid for the work they do.

Many people think this is necessary to get their foot in the door for certain jobs and industries, but there's no need for you to work full-time for a company and not be paid. It's not fair on you and is not a necessity to get a job.

But work experience does provide a whole host of great benefits towards improving your employment potential:

- **Practical experience** You might think you've learnt everything about your chosen career during your degree, but trust me – you won't have. It's not until you actually put the theories into practice that you get a proper view of the job itself. Work experience allows you to do this.
- **A foot in the door** Performing well on a work placement and impressing the people in charge can lead to offers of full-time employment. This happens more often than you might think. Regardless of whether the people you

work with can give you a job, the contacts you make might open other doors for you.

- **It might help you pass your degree** You might get your hands on some additional skills and information that the other people on your course just don't have! This can be applied directly to your studies, and if used in the right way can bump up your grades. This in turn will give you a better chance of getting a job in the long run.

So, you may be thinking, it's all well and good telling me about how useful doing work experience is, but how in hell do I go about getting some? Well, let me tell you the best places (and ways) to start:

- **University Careers Service** As with everything else careers-related, your first port of call should be your university careers office. Go to a careers adviser or someone on your campus who handles work placements and ask them to hook you up with one (or at least point you in the right direction). They'll probably have a database of possible placements, and they should help you get what you're looking for.
- **Specialist websites** There are sites that just do work experience stuff and they'll do all the hard work for you. For example, Fledglings.net does just that. You can narrow down searches to location and the area you want to work in, and a list of available placements will pop up for you. Simple!
- **Write to a company** It's not hard to find a company's contact details these days. Get these and drop them an email. The worst that can happen is they ignore you or say no, and the best is that they offer you some work experience. If your email doesn't work, don't give up – give them a call. I recommend ringing them anyway as this will connect you with someone straight away, without the delay of waiting for a reply. If this fails you can always go there. This could show you as being keen, and as someone with initiative and confidence. It could also make them think you're a stalker, but it could be worth the risk.

Searching for a job

I'd like to be able to say that there are loads of jobs out there, but we all know that's not the case. And if you want to find one of the jobs that are, you need to know where to look. It's like anything in life – if you look in the wrong places you're never going to find what you're looking for.

You should expect the job-hunting process to be a highly pressurised one. Expect to be hit with a high level of uncertainty and pressure from your family to get to work. When you start seeing your friends getting jobs it'll be tempting to just throw in the towel and give up. But you have to just suck it up and get on with the search.

Luckily there are plenty of places you can start (and continue) your job search:

■ **University careers office** Yes, this has been mentioned several times, but your university careers office is the best place to start when looking for anything to do with your career. They'll be able to advise you where to start your job search and should have details of available vacancies.

■ **Campus careers fairs** Count the times you've walked straight past those people from some company advertising their careers on campus. I bet it's quite a few. Next time, stop and talk to them. You might open the door to an amazing career opportunity simply by taking a few minutes to have a chat – even if you're not directly interested in what they have to offer.

■ **Jobcentre Plus** This is essentially a government service whose sole purpose is to find people like you a job. Their advisers can tell you about local jobs and other ones all over the country. Once you find a position that sounds

good to you, they'll help you apply and, if they can, they'll even give the employer a call there and then and arrange an interview. If not they'll send you an application form. Visit www.gov.uk/contact-jobcentre-plus

■ **The web** You can find everything on the Internet, and that includes jobs. There are loads of sites that specialise in jobs listings. On these you can filter what you're looking for by position, region, and even how much you want to earn. These are also useful for researching what's out there. A few good sites for students and graduates are:
— www.graduate-jobs.com
— www.indeed.co.uk
— www.prospects.ac.uk
— www.milkround.com

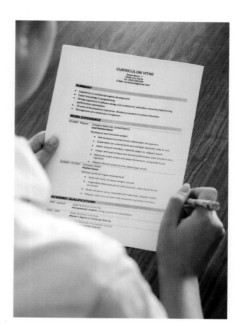

■ **Social media** People are regularly getting jobs by networking on social media. For example, using LinkedIn can help you create and add to a network of people, who are in turn part of a larger network of people who all have the potential to get you a job. Your social media persona can act as a great advertisement for yourself, and done right can be an amazing platform to showcase your work and skills. But always act with caution. Make sure your social media profile is clean for work – that picture of you passed-out amongst a pile of drunk, nude people won't send out the right message.

■ **Industry magazines** Most industry magazines are crammed full of jobs. A magazine like *New Scientist* often has its final third devoted to jobs (often graduate ones). Find a magazine focussed on your career area (if there is

one) and sift through the jobs available. Often such magazines have dedicated job sections on their website for you to take a look at too.

■ **Newspapers** This might sound old fashioned now, but a lot of employers (especially big and exciting ones) still use newspapers (and magazines) to advertise their positions. Free-sheets often have positions towards the back, and many publications have specific days when they carry a jobs supplement. I always picked up *The Guardian* on a Monday for their media jobs supplement, for example.

■ **The company** Why not contact the company direct to see if they have any vacancies? You've nothing to lose. Yes, it might annoy them if you call them daily asking for a job, but a simple polite enquiry can show you being proactive and give you information about a job that they're not widely advertising.

CV tips

In the battle for jobs your first line of attack is your CV. If you have a bad CV you really have no chance of getting a job. It represents you, the very best of you. It's there to show an employer that not only can you do the job, but you can do it well. Employers are generally interested in the following bits of information:

- Your contact details and relevant personal information.
- Your education.
- Your work experience.
- Your interests.
- Two referees who can vouch for how good you are.

Other things an employer might be looking for are:

- Achievements.
- Sports.
- Volunteering.
- Skills.

Here are some simple tips to make sure your CV stands out:

Make it easy for the employer to find the information they're most interested in. Split it down under simple headings; use bullet-points and keep the information to the point.

Make your CV unique for each position. Make sure each version of your CV plays to your strengths for that position – structure it so that the most relevant points and experience are on show. Remember, not all experience will be applicable to each position – your paper round when you were 12 isn't impressive for a job in banking!

Make it no longer than two pages – no one wants to read loads of text when they have hundreds of CVs to go through.

Make sure it's presented in an easily readable font.

Developer, Software Company, July 1994 – Novem

Within this role, I had sole responsibility for design a Geographical Information System (GIS). I success the requirements of various business objectives.

Graduate Software Engineer, Computer Com

I successfully completed first two years of ac all necessary work placements to all aspect redeveloping Graduate Training Scheme, a Engineering Project Team.

Education

Postgraduate College 1991
Institute of Technology

2.1 BA (Hons) in Software Engi
Jobsville University

2 S levels grade I and II, 198
5 A Levels grade A, 1987
Jobsville High School

References

John Doe
Chief Technical Offic

Software Compan
House

Ann Another

Address

10 High Street
Jobsville

Telephone

01234 567890

Objective

To obtain employment as a software developer in

Highlights

- 9 years IT development experience
- Friendly, flexible, and pro-active manne
- Successful at customer facing work
- Flair for creativity and design
- Extensive Internet and Intranet devel

Employment History

Software Developer, Computer Company

I am a key member in the software team re
internet search technology. I have develo
applications covering all stage
responsible for pro

CURRICULUM VITAE

Interviews

So, your CV has caught an employer's eye and they've offered you an interview. This is it, your chance to impress them enough that they want to start paying you.

Types of job interview

Although they all aim to do exactly the same thing there are a few different types of interview that you can be subjected to:

- **Competency-based interview** Here you'll need to talk about the skills you have and how they apply to the job. You'll have to explain what you've achieved in the past using the relevant skills. Try to illustrate your skills with practical examples.
- **Technical interview** You'll be asked and expected to answer technical questions about the job. You might even be asked to complete a small task to show your understanding of the technical side of the business. Not knowing everything isn't a bad thing, this will simply inform the company that you need some additional training in some areas.
- **Portfolio-based interview** These are most common for jobs in media and fashion, where you'll be expected to present a portfolio. In most cases no portfolio will mean no job!
- **Group interview** This type of interview is aimed at seeing how good you are at teamwork. Often companies who work in teams will hold group interviews for applicants. These can be tricky, as you want to show that you're outgoing and motivational but without overpowering. So leave your ego at the door.
- **Telephone interview** Preliminary nterviews can be conducted over the phone or video call. You'll need to be more professional on the phone as you won't have the benefit of facial cues and body language.

What to do in a job interview

It's easy to make a good impression but just as easy to make it go horribly wrong. Here's what to consider when getting ready for a job interview:

- **Be early** Arrive around 15 minutes early. This will show that you're punctual, and give you time to relax a bit. The last thing you want to do is arrive in a sweaty, panting mess.
- **Turn it off** Whatever you do, make sure your phone is turned off, or at least on silent.
- **Looking professional: dos and don'ts** There are a lot of things you should and shouldn't do in an interview, and here are some basic remaining dos and don'ts:

DOS

- Enter the room with a smile on your face.
- Give a firm handshake.
- Introduce yourself while shaking hands.
- Look the interviewers in the eye.
- Look interested all the way through.
- Listen!
- Ask plenty of questions…
  …but don't interrupt, or ask questions that you've already heard the answer to.
- Give full answers (not just yes or no).
- Speak clearly.
- Give evidence when answering questions.
- Appear confident.
- Sit back with an upright posture.

DON'TS

- Lie! (Always always tell the truth, even if it's painful to do so.)
- Swear (even words you consider harmless).
- Criticise previous employers.
- Fold your arms when people are talking to you.
- Challenge authority.
- Talk about your weaknesses more than your strengths.
- Slouch.

Don't be scared to ask questions

If you're unsure what a question means, ask them to clarify it. It won't make you look incompetent; in fact it will show your attention to detail. Asking is definitely better than getting it wrong and giving a completely off the point answer.

How to leave

Shake the interviewers' hands, thank them for their time, and add that you look forward to hearing from them. Try to be friendly and confident – but don't overdo it.

Preparation is key

■ **Be prepared** Make sure you know everything you need to know. Consider the basics first – do you know where and when the interview is and how long you need to allow to get there in plenty of time?

■ **What do they do?** Research the company, what they do and what they expect. It will show that you're keen and really want the job if you know about them.

■ **Why do you want the job?** There's a high likelihood you'll be asked why you want the job. You should have thought out exactly why you do. Never say it was your second choice, or that you want it for the money. Explain how it fits in with your own personal goals; this can give you a good opportunity to dazzle them with some of your company knowledge.

■ **Know your skills** Sure, you already know what you're good at, but how do your skills apply to the job and how can they be applied to benefit the employer? Showing this will give you a much better chance of getting the job.

■ **Know the industry** Read up on all current affairs and news that could affect the company that's interviewing you, and, if possible, try to form an opinion on them. Showing that you're aware of and thinking about issues that the company faces will score you some serious points.

■ **Any questions?** You'll often be asked at the end of an interview if you have any questions. It's always good to have one or two relevant queries up your sleeve at this point, which shows you are genuinely interested and also helps to end the interview on a positive note.

Graduate schemes

Despite all the doom and gloom there's a great route into the graduate career that you seek. This is by graduate training schemes. They're offered by the top companies in most sectors and offer the brilliant combination of on-the-job training and a decent salary. In most cases these companies are looking to mould graduate talent into the business leaders of the future.

Salaries might not be as high as a normal full-time employee, but they're still good, and getting on one of these schemes is a definite foot in the door – chances of being kept on after the training scheme are very high. With these schemes usually lasting a year you'll be in employment proper before you know it.

The schemes are far from an easy ride, though. Companies invest a lot of time and money in them and so expect loyalty, dedication and focus once you're on the job. Expect to have to work long hours and very hard to prove yourself. If you think you can handle this straight out of uni, it's this 'proving yourself' which will bag you a sustained career.

The good thing is that as a trainee you can afford to make mistakes – at this point you're still learning the job and will be allowed to correct your mistakes, often under the guidance and support of a mentor.

Regardless of whether you stay with the company or not, the training and experience you've gained will give you transferable skills and boost your confidence, and when it comes to getting another job it'll make negotiating more money much easier.

It might sound perfect, but committing to a graduate scheme at a particular company shouldn't be a decision you take lightly. Do your research and ask yourself what it is you want and what kind of career you're looking for in the long run.

Getting yourself on a graduate scheme

Graduate schemes sound great, don't they? This is why they're very, very popular, and competition is really high to bag a place on one. But there are a few ways of making sure you can stay ahead of the pack.

It's a good idea to start early. The best time to apply is at least a year before you graduate, as this is the time when companies tend to snap up people for the next year's scheme.

You should keep a close eye on application deadlines. Most bigger recruiters end their process in January; some may continue the process till May, but these tend to be smaller companies with less positions on offer.

Applying while still at university also gives you the added benefit of being able to ask your university careers office for help and guidance. The careers offices will have loads of information on employers, what they offer and what the requirements are to get on their schemes.

Aside from your careers office there are lots of places to find out about graduate schemes – keep your eyes peeled for posters and stalls on campus, and make sure you attend one of the many graduate careers fairs running throughout the country.

It's worth having a few copies of your CV on you at these careers fairs. Being able to hand over your details to a company representative might give you an advantage and get you a much desired phone call.

Obviously, traditional means like looking through newspapers and careers-orientated magazines are still good ways to find out about schemes, but these days the Internet is the best place to find info at any time. All top recruiters have a website and will have details of their graduate schemes on it. Even if you just happen to have a quick glance at these companies at a fair or elsewhere on campus, you can follow up to find out more online.

Once you've found which scheme you want to get on you have to actually apply. This scares a lot of people silly, but it's really nothing to worry about. Make your CV and any other supporting material focus on the position. Most companies aren't really interested in your basic educational skills but are keen on other skills that make you stand apart from the crowd. Highlight the skills you have and what makes you special. Each company will have their own slightly different application requirements, so make sure you've properly fulfilled all of these. Don't simply try and write a 'one size fits all' application if you're trying for a place on several schemes.

If you get through to the interview stages, make sure you present yourself professionally. Don't turn up in jeans and a T-shirt. Guys should go for a shirt and tie, trousers and shoes. Girls should also go for a smart look. Answer all questions honestly and be confident – if you've been asked in for an interview they must think you have the right skills to get the job.